manage your stress

Trusted Advice for a Healthier Life
from Harvard Medical School

Manage your Stress

Overcoming Stress in the Modern World

Joseph Shrand, MD
with Leigh M. Devine, MS

St. Martin's Paperbacks

The information in this book is not intended to replace the advice of the reader's own physician or other medical professional. You should consult a medical professional in matters relating to health, especially if you have existing medical conditions, and before starting, stopping or changing the dose of any medication you are taking. Individual readers are solely responsible for their own health care decisions. The author and the publisher do not accept responsibility for any adverse effects individuals may claim to experience, whether directly or indirectly, from the information contained in this book.

The fact that an organization or web site is mentioned in the book as a potential source of information does not mean that the author or the publisher endorse any of the information it may provide or recommendations it may make.

The stories in this book are composite, fictional accounts based on the experiences of many individuals. Similarities to any real person or persons are coincidental and unintentional.

MANAGE YOUR STRESS

Copyright © 2012 by Harvard University.

For information address St. Martin's Press, 175 Fifth Avenue, New York, NY 10010.

EAN: 978-1-250-00854-1

Printed in the United States of America

St. Martin's Paperbacks edition / July 2012

St. Martin's Paperbacks are published by St. Martin's Press, 175 Fifth Avenue, New York, NY 10010.

10 9 8 7 6 5 4 3 2 1

To my departed loved ones:
My dad, Hyman Shrand, my mom, Frances Shrand,
and my sister, Susan Shrand.
I miss the way you helped me.
—JOSEPH

To my mother, Elaine Fraser Devine.
—LEIGH

contents

acknowledgments

I'd like to acknowledge the following people for helping make this book become a reality:

Julie Silver, MD, Chief Editor in Books at Harvard Health Publications, who conceived the idea for this project and assembled the author team. I thank you for your tireless patience and advocacy.

Tony Komaroff, MD, Editor-in-Chief of Harvard Health Publications. I appreciate your passion for bringing to the public medical information that is practical, accessible, and accurate.

Linda Konner, my literary agent. Your ability to shape a project and bring all parties to the table is unparalleled.

Meredith Mennitt, my wonderful St. Martin's Press editor who diplomatically helped guide me through the book-writing process and made these pages all the better for it.

My friend writer Leigh Devine who kept the blinkers on me when I would stray.

My wife and vitamin C, Carol Shrand, who made writing a book on stress about as stress free as it could be, as well as my kids, Sophie, Jason, Galen, and Becca Mai, whose willingness to help their mom was critical in keeping down the cortisol levels at home.

The many scientists, researchers, colleagues, and patients who contributed to the wealth of information and the truth of this book: living their own examples of our ancient limbic logics, and their ability to keep it frontal in times of tension.

—Joseph Shrand, MD

What Is Stress?

chapter 1

A Response to Your World

For nearly a decade Jennifer supported herself and four kids as a shrimp-net maker. But after the oil-rig explosion in 2010 shut down Gulf fishing, Jennifer couldn't find other work and was forced to accept charity for the first time. Her hardest moments came at Christmas when she had little to give her children. While things had been tough before, Jennifer recalls that her stress level was at least manageable. "If I only had to worry about my car breaking down here and there, I'd still be pretty happy," she said.

For all of us, stress comes in many different packages. Jennifer's latest stress has been brought on by a sudden, negative change in circumstances. For others, stress comes on in a traumatic way such as a car accident or death of a loved one. But routine, chronic stress that is related to work pressures, family life, and other responsibilities can, in the long run, lead to serious physical and mental health consequences if not managed properly. And this kind of stress can sneak up on you quietly and gradually.

If you've picked up this book because you're thinking that stress may be getting the better of you—or possibly even making you sick—then you are in good company. As the ripple effect of the Great Recession is still being felt across the country, people are reporting both high levels of daily stress as well as acutely stressful events, brought on by the nation's economic woes. According to the American Psychological Association's Stress in America 2010 survey, 76 percent of the respondents cited money concerns as the number one source of stress, followed by work at 70 percent, and worries about the general economy at 65 percent. Despite their awareness of the source, only a third of those surveyed said they were doing a good job managing their stress. And the majority of children whose parents endure very high levels of stress say there is a negative impact on their families.

While it is inevitable that human beings are going to be faced with many types of stressful events throughout a lifetime—from traumatic events to daily irritants—what is not a given is how we respond to those events. We can reduce the impact of stress in our lives and on our health by understanding why we experience stress, what is going on in our brain and body, and how, in fact, we cannot live safely *without* stress.

Your Perception of Stress Triggers

Many people describe their stress in concrete and common ways such as work deadlines, rude drivers, argumentative coworkers, a stack of unpaid bills, being evaluated. The feelings you experience at these times tend to be negative, can put you in a bad mood, or even worse, make you angry and aggressive.

But if you look at these scenarios as a third party or a medical expert, you would see how these instances are actually individual causes or sources of the stress experience. We call them *stressors* or *triggers*. In general, they come in two varieties:

1. common, daily occurrences that grind down on your patience, or
2. unexpected events that seem to conspire against you before you've even gotten to work

You feel like you've been mentally and physically put through the wringer and, in a way, you really have. Your body has reacted to the event of being cut off in traffic almost in the same way as if a rhinoceros had charged you. When you experience a stress trigger your heart beats quickly, your palms and body sweat, blood rushes to your face, and your breathing quickens. Some stress makes us just want to run away or hide. Other times people feel charged, ready to fight after the event has passed. Sometimes people feel exhausted by it, or overwhelmed. Whatever your instinctive feeling may be in those moments, it is what you choose to *do* right after that stress moment that can mean the difference between a ruined or normal day.

All too often we continue to let our fear or anger from a stress trigger stew and feed upon itself. We focus on the event, replaying it, telling it to others. Few of us are taught that what is actually happening in our minds and bodies during a stress trigger is a perfectly normal and protective physiological event. Having the tools to cope and calm ourselves when we are confronted by either a chronically stressful job, or a sudden negative event will make a big difference when we experience the stress response.

In order to understand why we respond to triggers—and it happens to all of us automatically—it helps to look at the human brain and the mechanisms that trigger our stress responses. This journey takes us deep into the central workings of the human neuroendocrine system, which is responsible for the delicate interplay between our brain and the chemicals and hormones that influence how we react and respond to the world around us. Once you begin to learn about why our bodies do what they do, you'll see how stress is a useful partner in life. Without it, we could not have survived as a species.

chapter 2
_____

Biological Origins of Stress

Stress and Survival Go Together

If you've ever seen the film classic *Jurassic Park*, you will remember the heart-pounding scenes where several characters were being chased over the fields by those ferocious velociraptors. Those characters were dramatizing what our evolutionary ancestors no doubt experienced—the need to literally run for your life. While we don't get chased by many reptiles in the modern world, our bodies still react to threats in a similar and automatic way.

It's all about evolution. Hardwired into every mammal's brain is an apparatus for automatic and unconscious scanning of our surroundings—assessing for danger, safety, predators, and much more. There is little doubt that during evolution, there was a survival advantage to having such an efficient safety system in place. The creature that paid no attention to that rustling in the bush became lunch much more often than the creature that recognized the danger and did something. Reacting to the danger bestowed the best chance of survival. Once the brain perceived a danger, the body took action; to attack or defend, run away, or try to hide and become invisible until the danger had passed. Negotiation was not an option.

These days it is unlikely that we will be eaten by a hungry predator. But our ancient brains still respond the way they have for millions of years. Of course, in today's world we have many different kinds of stressors. Instead of having four legs, they often have four wheels or rechargeable batteries. When we are confronted with a stressor—which could be any real or imagined stimulus that requires us to change or act quickly—we feel the inner sensation of our bodies going into an instant, hyperactive mode. Think of what happens to you when you even *think* something dangerous is about to happen. You become *startled*. A car pulls out in front of you unexpectedly. A door slams when no one else is home. You lock your keys in the car. The muscles tense, the heart pounds. We all know intimately how this feels.

This is our neuroendocrine system jolting into action, triggering the release of specialized hormones that produce those sudden and well-orchestrated physiological changes that create the stress response. Exactly how and why these reactions occur and what effects they might have on us over time are questions that have intrigued researchers for years.

Fight, Flight, and the Frightened Cats

Harvard physiologist Walter B. Cannon was a pioneer in exploring the biochemistry of the stress response. His research nearly a century ago convinced him that fright was not all in the mind, but also stemmed from the adrenal glands, two tiny hat-shaped structures sitting atop the kidneys. To test his theory, Cannon set up an experiment in which he caused dogs to bark menacingly at caged cats. He was then able to isolate a hormone secreted by the adrenal glands of the frightened cats. When he injected that hormone into a second, perfectly calm cat, it touched off a fear reaction. The cat's heartbeat and blood pressure shot up, while the muscles enjoyed an increase in blood flow. Cannon called this occurrence the *fight-or-flight-or-freeze* response.

These days, we call it simply the *fight or flight* or the *stress response*. From a survival point of view it makes perfect sense: If you are in danger, you want to send as much energy as possible, in the form of oxygen and sugars carried by blood, to the muscles of your arms and legs so you can either flee, or be prepared to fight for your life. By studying these frightened felines, Cannon had uncovered a critical insight into the stress response: the role of hormones.

The initial stress hormone Cannon isolated was something called *epinephrine.* You might recognize the name, especially if you have or know a child with severe food allergies. An *Epipen,* now a common item in school classrooms to mediate severe allergic reaction, is named after the hormone it administers. Epinephrine pushes open the airways in the lungs. More commonly, we call this hormone *adrenaline,* after the glands that manufacture it. Cannon also discovered a second stress-response hormone called *norepinephrine,* or *noradrenaline,* which makes your heart rate and blood pressure soar during a fight-or-flight reaction. A sudden, rapid rise of norepinephrine is what also causes panic attacks. Other researchers later discovered a third crucial hormone of the stress response, *cortisol* (what I refer to as the "Minutemen"), which further prepares the body to fight or flee by increasing blood sugar to provide energy, suppressing the immune system, and shutting down the digestive system.

Think about what we needed to be able to do if faced with a threat. We would first need to recognize we were in danger. To do this, certain parts of your brain had to remain continually vigilant. At the same time our brain needed to process the meaning of what we observed, as well as look for changes in that environment, such as an approaching animal. After assessing the strength of that animal, your brain would begin to mobilize the body.

In less than a heartbeat, the chemical messenger corticotropin-releasing factor (CRF), what I call the "Paul Revere" of hormones, gets released from your hypothalamus and courses down a neural pathway to the nearby pituitary gland.

As if in a chemical relay race, the pituitary cells then send their own chemical messenger, adrenocorticotropic hormone (ACTH), to the adrenal glands, which mobilize the "Minutemen" of our defenses, spilling cortisol into the bloodstream. Cortisol, the critical stress hormone, helps to convert fats into easy-to-access sugars: the energy we need to run away or stand and fight. Surges of adrenaline and noradrenaline are also released by the adrenal glands on instructions from the brain and simultaneously throughout the body by the sympathetic nervous system. Scientists call this powerful triumvirate of the hypothalamus, pituitary gland, and adrenal glands the *HPA axis*.

This cocktail of stress hormones races through your bloodstream to different parts of your body, preparing you to fight or flee. Your breath quickens as your body

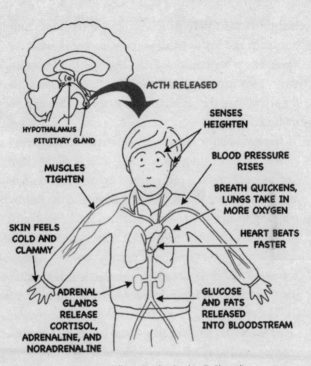

HYPOTHALAMUS
PITUITARY GLAND

ACTH RELEASED

SENSES
HEIGHTEN

BLOOD PRESSURE
RISES

MUSCLES
TIGHTEN

BREATH QUICKENS,
LUNGS TAKE IN
MORE OXYGEN

SKIN FEELS
COLD AND
CLAMMY

HEART BEATS
FASTER

ADRENAL
GLANDS
RELEASE
CORTISOL,
ADRENALINE, AND
NORADRENALINE

GLUCOSE
AND FATS
RELEASED
INTO BLOODSTREAM

Figure 1: Stress Response (Illustration by Sophia T. Shrand)

takes in extra oxygen. Energy-boosting glucose and fats are released from storage sites into your bloodstream. Sharpened senses, such as sight and hearing, prepare you to detect changes in your surroundings and respond rapidly. Your heart beats faster, up to two to three times as quickly as normal. Your blood pressure rises. Certain blood vessels constrict, directing blood flow to your muscles and brain and away from your organs and skin, something we have all experienced in the form of cold sweats.

Simultaneously, specialized blood cells, called platelets, become stickier, so clots can form more easily to minimize bleeding from potential injuries. The immune system goes into high gear to fight bacteria from possible bites and scratches. Your muscles—even the tiny, hair-raising muscles beneath your skin—tighten, preparing you to spring into action. Body systems not needed for the immediate emergency are suppressed. The stomach and intestines cease operations. Sexual arousal lessens. Repair and growth of body tissues slows. In essence, without being fully aware of how you are doing it, you have primed yourself to combat a perceived (real or imagined) attack.

When the danger passes, the body is designed to naturally bring itself back to that low-grade, seemingly unconscious state of vigilance. Indeed, Cannon believed the stress response was temporary. Minutes after the rush triggered by adrenaline, he thought the body would wind back down to its normal balance, a physical state known as *homeostasis*. Everything reverses and goes back to normal; heart rate and blood pressure; breathing and muscles; platelets and the immune system all go back to their previous state. Your intestines would start their work again, providing new fuel to replace the energy burned in the emergency. Bones would resume repairs or start growing again, and reproductive activity might appear more inviting. You have survived another day.

With the challenge that sparked the stress response behind you and the parasympathetic nervous system exerting its calming influence, the day-to-day business of your body would resume. However, current research has shown that this recovery does not always work as well as we'd like it to, especially among the many people who experience chronic stress. Those hormonal effects, so vital and heroic during times of fight or flee, can be detrimental to health when the body no longer needs them.

The Positive Side of Stress

Amid all our fears of stress, though, it's very important to recognize that the stress response can be enormously helpful. We can't live and function in the world without it. It is also the stress response that enables people to perform enormous and vital feats. Think about the life-saving work done by emergency workers and ordinary people confronted in accidents and disasters. When an elderly woman fell onto the New York City subway tracks, a plumber jumped down to grab her just as the train pulled into the station. His stress response saved her life and he was hailed a hero.

The fight-or-flight response can prove beneficial

under far less dangerous circumstances, too. Helping someone in need, such as a skier who suddenly falls in front of you, also activates your stress response. But recent studies have shown that people who acted to help and those who *received* help both had lower levels of cortisol in response to stress triggers. This suggests that when we help each other in times of stress we both benefit on a neurochemical basis. In the following chapters, we'll explore how you can use this information to better manage stress in your own life, and in the lives of others.

Stress has been the subject of scientific curiosity for more than a century now. The word *stress* derives from the Latin, *stringere,* meaning "to stretch." To Canadian physiologist and endocrinologist Hans Selye, who first popularized the concept of stress in the 1950s, the term suggested a stretching of physical and psychological resources to meet demands placed on an organism. Selye studied the line between short-term stress that stimulates people to persevere to overcome obstacles (*eustress,* or "good" stress) and chronic or excessive stress, which wears down the ability to adapt and cope (*distress,* or "bad" stress). But whether it was good or bad, he maintained, the impact on the body was identical. Selye was also the first to show the role of emotional responses in causing much of the wear and tear experienced by people throughout their lives.

But Selye was not the first to recognize that there

was indeed a positive side to the stress response. Research on the relationship between stress arousal and performance goes back more than hundred years to Robert Yerkes and John Dodson. In 1908, these two Harvard researchers wrote a landmark paper stating that as stress or anxiety levels rose, so did performance and efficiency—up to a point. At this turning point, further stress and anxiety led to significant declines in performance and ability—a concept still known as Yerkes–Dodson Law. Where that turning point occurs differs from person to person. For while the stress response is hardwired into all humans and other animals, the events and perceptions that set it off vary widely. What you perceive as a threatening situation, your neighbor, or even your spouse, may easily brush aside. Not all of us can handle working in an emergency room, diving near sharks, or scaling Mount Everest.

It turns out that stress-hardy people share several common characteristics. Researchers have found that exercise and social support proved essential. So did control, challenge, and commitment. Stress-hardy people have been found to feel a sense of control, or have the ability to influence events, embrace the challenge in situations others might find stressful, and describe themselves as committed to something meaningful. People with these attributes report fewer illnesses and are less likely to be absent from work.

The ability to think on your feet is another trait common to stress-hardy people, according to a 2010 study in the journal *Psychology and Aging*. Twelve-hundred people between the ages of forty-five to sixty-nine were asked about their positive and negative mood status for that day. They also completed a test that measured what the researchers called their *fluid cognitive ability*—the participants' ability to use reason quickly and think abstractly. Those with higher levels of fluid cognitive ability, they found, were associated with greater exposure to work- and home-related stress overloads. Ironically, this group, who reported the highest amount of small stressors, reported a lower level of negative moods. Meanwhile, those who scored lowest on their fluid cognitive ability, experienced the opposite, which may indicate that some people are more easily overwhelmed by the stress response and so are less able to think quickly and more apt to experience more negative moods. Stress, it appears, can rob people of their ability to think.

These findings unfortunately beg the question of what exactly controls one's ability to weather the stress response. It would seem that the stress response interferes with some people's brain function as well as their ability to manage negative moods. On the other hand, a certain amount of stress helps some people perform better, leading to a decrease in negative moods. What is certain is that further study of what makes the stress-hardy so resilient is much needed.

For the vast majority of us, the experience of being in constant, revved-up survival mode is not just unpleasant but physically and mentally unsustainable. Chronic stress, which can lead to what I've nicknamed a "cortisol marinade," may cause unnecessary wear on the body as well as a myriad of debilitating conditions including anxiety and depression. Stress can trigger flare-ups of asthma, rheumatoid arthritis, and gastrointestinal problems, such as irritable bowel syndrome.

Stress affects you emotionally as well, stealing joy from your life and all it has to offer. Life is just not as much fun if your brain always perceives the worst.

My interest in stress stems in part from my own childhood. My mother was an actress and my father a pediatrician. They did not have a happy marriage and divorced when I was fourteen. The stress at home was often intense, as my parents battled each other over often long-forgotten insults. The daily barrage of conflict interfered with their lives, my schoolwork, and their happiness. During the divorce I saw how much damage can be done when you have no means to resolve that much stress. The arguing and blaming impacted both my parents' lives for as long as they lived. But it also created in me a determination to explore this stress response, and try to develop a way for others to at least have some tools to combat this deeply ingrained re-action to the world around us.

As a psychiatrist I have the amazing privilege of being with people at a time of need. As a child psychiatrist in particular, I see how multigenerational conflicts can permeate their way into the lives of a child, even if the child themselves is an innocent bystander of the stress of their parents. Not that stress is a sin, but in a very real way, the proverbial "sins of the father" (and mother), do play out in the lives of the child. But what I have been fascinated by is the myriad of responses people have to this ubiquitous event in our everyday lives. Not all of these are unhealthy, but many can lead to significant stress in and of themselves.

For example, some children are more resilient to stress, and take this ramped-up cortisol response to excel in school, sports, and creative process. But others are not so adept. In my current position I work with adolescents who have begun using drugs and alcohol. Many of them use in response to the stress of life. Those who got hooked into the limbic world of addiction, create stress which is then compounded in them, their families, and communities, by the very substance they were using to relieve the stress they were experiencing. Others were from good homes, but were at a party where drugs and alcohol were passed around for so-called "fun." But those who got seduced by these substances created the same stress as those who were already seeking an escape. Stress can insidiously germinate and create more stress until it seems overwhelming.

This is why I have written this book. To help the reader understand what this stress thing is all about, to share some of my own experiences in helping people, and to assure you that stress is a normal part of being human. Stress itself is adaptive and useful, a part of the survival tool kit we have evolved over millions of years. It is what you do with your stress, or what unbridled stress can do to you, that is the real danger. Stress can be an instrument of success or a weapon of significant destruction.

It's never too late to learn to address the seemingly endless stressors in the world today. You can take control over how you react to stress and learn to better manage your mental and physical reactions, and I will help you get started in the following chapters. So relax, and read on.

part II

Understanding Your Stress

chapter 3

Key Sources of Stress

All through dinner Beth tried in vain to get her young sons to eat their chicken nuggets. She tried coaxing and pleading. Her husband then tried bribing with dessert. The boys just fidgeted and fought. It was the last thing Beth needed to top off a hectic, ten-hour workday. After dinner, she cleared the table and asked her husband to take out the trash. When he didn't respond after the second request, she found herself screaming the third time. *Why did dinner have to be so complicated?!* Her heart raced as she breathed in, squelching the urge to throw a glass against the wall.

If you stop and think about what we reviewed in the last chapter about fight or flight, then it might seem odd that Beth would react nearly as intensely to her sons' bad behavior as she might to their lives being threatened. But actually it may not be so odd considering the way our brain has been designed for survival. What is different today is that we perceive our basic survival as dependent on things like electricity, being on time for meetings, and, for some, our kids eating their chicken nuggets. In a sense, we have transferred our survival-based stress response to entities that have little to do with real survival and all to do with conveniences of, and control over, modern life. Sadly, in the process of this we're not only robbing ourselves of joy, but also making ourselves sick.

So how does knowing about stress help us to better manage stress and balance the good stress with the bad? By getting to know our many stress triggers, as well as those of people around us, we can recognize and over-ride our urge to fight or flee, anticipate how our body will react, and take steps to remain calm and reflective— and not *reflexive*. For instance, if you know your kids might not always be hungry at dinnertime, you are less likely to let those very predictable triggers get the best of you, as they did poor Beth. A kid who is not hungry is not a predator that is.

Stress at Home

Of all the places where we expect to feel free of stress, the home can instead be a minefield of stress triggers, especially for working parents like Beth who juggle the demands of the workplace for the better part of the day and then come home to face the needs of children, partners, and pets, not to mention the household items that constantly need to be cleaned and fixed. For many people, work actually feels like the escape. At work most people have to be concerned only with themselves. At home, there are many relationships to manage and many opportunities for stress. In fact, with the four people in Beth's family, there are thirteen relationship combinations around a small dinner table. Each of these relationships and individuals brings their own needs, desires, and sources of stress into the family dynamic every single day:

1. Beth, her husband, and the two kids
2. Beth, her husband, and one kid
3. Beth, her husband, and the other kid
4. Beth and both kids
5. Beth and her husband
6. Beth by herself
7. Husband and both kids
8. Husband and one kid
9. Husband and the other kid
10. Husband by himself
11. Eldest kid and other kid
12. Eldest kid by himself
13. Youngest kid by himself

Take a list like this and apply it to your own life. As you can see, with every relationship set, there are many potential sources of stress. But along with the multitude of home triggers, there are also many mechanisms that help alleviate stress among couples and families. It may sound like common sense, but couples that are satisfied with their marriages have been shown to have lower levels of the stress hormone, cortisol. University of California researchers reported in a 2010 *Journal of Personality and Social Psychology* study that the cortisol level of couples actually influenced each other. When one partner was in a negative mood, the presence of their partner alleviated this both psychologically and hormonally indicating that happier couples may indeed have calmer homes and vice versa.

Perhaps if Beth's husband had been more of a team player during the dinnertime routine, it is possible that Beth's stress levels would have been modulated by his supportive actions. If Beth and her husband's marriage was a happy one, this would increase the likelihood that their home became a place where their relationship would become a buffer against the other stress triggers brought on through the remaining family stress combinations. Helping each other out is a way to decrease stress.

But even if Beth's marriage wasn't so good, *any* emotional support could help diffuse a stress trigger as well as improve someone's mood. Positive emotions have been shown to either protect against stress, or reduce the response to stress according to numerous scientific studies. Other findings indicate that feeling supported actually increases oxytocin levels. Oxytocin, a hormone associated with attachment and a sense of well-being, has also been found to help the healing process and possibly protect against disease according to recent data from a research team at the University of Southern California.

It almost sounds too simple, but really learning to be proactive and providing positive support to family members may go a long way toward arming us emotionally for the other stress triggers that lay ahead in our daily lives, especially in the places where we spend the greatest proportion of time—at work and at school.

Stress at Work

On a daily basis, most of us face a multiplicity of external stress triggers that are completely out of our control, as do Beth and her husband. From traffic, to weather, to bad service at the luncheonette. A major stressor of course comes from the places and people with whom we spend the most time, such as at our work and colleagues. This goes for men and women alike. In fact, we spend more time working than in previous decades and pervasive modern technology in the form of e-mail and "CrackBerries" is eroding the barrier that used to exist between our work and home life. While these devices are supposed to increase convenience, we are also learning just how much they may be increasing stress levels.

So what exactly was happening during the ten-hour workday that contributed to Beth's stress levels? Maybe she had an unrealistic deadline, equipment failures causing delays, or impending layoffs. If Beth was a mid-level manager, she had pressure coming from both ends of the spectrum. Some things may be under her control, while others certainly are not. In fact, a major determinant of how much work stress we experience is whether or not we feel in *control* of our time at all.

How much control do you have over your work? Do you get the support you need to do your job? Do you have flexible hours? Do you feel respected by colleagues and superiors? These are especially important points to examine in your work life, and research is pointing to how these control factors affect your stress levels, which in turn can affect your health.

For instance, in a major four-year British study of 21,300 female registered nurses, researchers found that those reporting minimal control over their jobs, little social support at work, and high job demands were more likely to be in poor health at the study's outset. They also suffered greater functional declines during the next four years. In this landmark study, published in the *British Medical Journal* ten years ago, job control depended on the worker's ability to acquire and apply new skills on the job and to have decision-making authority. Those with the highest control and lowest demands stayed healthiest.

Not surprisingly, job stress and heart disease have been linked in a growing body of research. In another major study, from the University of London, which involved ten thousand London-based male and female civil servants, scientists found that chronic work stress was associated with increased coronary artery disease, especially among people under age fifty. Other findings showed associations between work stress and low physical activity, poor diet, the metabolic syndrome including high blood pressure and insulin levels, and lower heart rate variability. Also among this group, work stress was associated with a higher morning rise in cortisol. High levels of cortisol most often mean high levels of stress.

We've been reminded during the recent economic downturn that what can be equally stressful to a difficult job is the stress of not working at all. This creates a whole other realm of anxiety that involves financial and marital pressures. I have seen many individuals for whom stress has grown into full-blown depression after being laid off. One man's comment in particular summed it up. Once a high-level and highly paid executive with a global chemical company, he did not survive a final round of management layoffs. "When someone asks me what I do for a living, I first feel sheer panic," he said. "But alone it turns to sorrow. I feel useless, worthless. Sometimes even helpless." Along with a severance package, one of the best send-off items that folks like this could use might just be a stress-anticipation-and-reduction plan. A person's very health could depend on it. Luckily for Beth, at least for now, her job appears safe. But how safe are her kids feeling in school?

Stress at School

Like the home and work for adults, school can be a hotbed of stress for our kids—at all ages. There are two main categories of relationships a kid needs to traverse at school: the one with their peers, and the one with their teachers and other administrative adults. When kids are very young, their first major stress trigger often comes when the parent leaves them at daycare or school for the first time. They have entered the world of other grown-ups; strangers much bigger and more powerful who have an influence on their daily lives—out of the direct sight of their parents. Separation anxiety is real. While it appears that some kids are having a tantrum at the thought of being separated from the parent, many are having full-blown, cortisol-fueled panic attacks. You've seen it and some of you have no doubt lived it. Once the child develops a bond with the teacher and classmates, however, the anxiety usually eases and eventually they skip off to class happily.

Many of us assume that the instructor's emotional support will help buffer a child's fear and stress. We encourage a warm feeling between our kids and teachers, often bringing a gift for the teacher to show they are special people in our kids' lives. It turns out that a positive teacher–pupil relationship is actually crucial, especially for youngsters. Researchers from the University of Wisconsin followed a group of kids from first grade and then evaluated them again in seventh grade. The results of their study were sobering. The kids who felt closer to their teachers fared better from a long-term mental health perspective than the kids who felt more distant.

Although the home environment must contribute in some way to our kids' stress levels and how they feel, the relationship with teachers can be independently influential. From my work with children and adolescents, it appears that all children (and this goes for adults, too) want to feel valued by another human being and not just Mom and Dad. We enjoy feeling valuable to anyone. Feeling valuable can lessen stress and cortisol, leads to improved self-value, and, at least in the Wisconsin study, less difficulty with mental health issues, most of which interfere with further human relationships.

Conversely, when teachers are overly critical and disapproving, this can create a long-lasting negative impact on a child's ability to form relationships, and to learn. While the vast majority of teachers are supportive of their students, the effect of just one teacher who is demeaning can still have an enormous and deleterious effect. This was the surprising, and disturbing discovery of psychologists from the University of Oregon who studied behaviors among a group of 241 local schoolchildren, starting in kindergarten. Most were succeeding socially and academically. Among those who were not, all had ongoing conflicts with their teachers; a trend that the researchers found persisted through elementary school. What is worrisome about these findings is the long shadow that this conflict may cast. It doesn't appear to matter who the teachers may be later on, the pattern of how a child views his or her relationship with the teacher appears to be established very early and consistently.

What if one of Beth's children is having a hard time building trust and a good relationship with the teacher? Or perhaps one of the kids was disciplined that day and still felt stressed out. With kids, events at school can be just as hard to leave behind as work stress at the office is for adults. Being yelled at by their mother later on can compound the stress the kids are already feeling. When the child doesn't eat, Beth and her husband may view this action as a rejection of them, and a disrespect of their authority, which makes them both angry. Beth's own stress may interfere with her ability to more accurately analyze the motivation behind the behavior of her kids and an opportunity to be supportive may be missed. Do you see how these family relationship combinations interact and sometimes become combustible due to stress in everyone's lives? But Beth's kid may have lost his appetite at home due to stress at school. Blood flow is diverted from the gut in the flight-fight stress response. Why eat if you fear being eaten.

As kids get older, however, some of the most stressful aspects of going to school become the social pressures, especially the need to fit into a social group. The fear of group exclusion and even worse, of being bullied, has only increased in recent years with the rampant proliferation of text messaging among kids. I personally find this to be a frightening trend and have seen the damaging effects of bullying among adolescents in my practice. The stress experienced by those being bullied can lead to physical problems, such as headaches and stomachaches. Bullying can lead to poor self-esteem, lack of friends, depression, anxiety, suicidal thoughts, and tragically, even suicide itself. Might the stress and fear of being bullied also be a reason that Beth's kids weren't hungry at dinner?

Strong family support can offer protection from the negative effects of bullying, and there is increasing evidence that positive home environments increase resiliency in children who have already been subjected to bullying. In a recent study in Finland, scientists gave questionnaires to nearly eight hundred children—first at the age of ten, and then again at age fourteen. They found that the children who felt they got along with their parents, and could communicate well with them, also reported being more satisfied with themselves, enjoying school more, feeling less lonely, being less bullied by others, and also bullying others less. It is the unfortunate truth that if Beth's kids are not getting along with her and their father, this could also be having a major impact on their school lives.

This is important information, because sometimes the effect of being bullied as a child can last a lifetime. Not only this, but research has recently shown that adults who had experienced being bullied while at school also reported a lower health-related quality of life as adults—another reason to get the stress under control among all family members as early and as consistently as possible. A kid who feels bullied does not feel valuable, leading to more vulnerability to stress.

It may be a struggle for parents to communicate

with their kids, especially teens. I know this challenge as I have two teens myself, and two older kids that were teens. The proliferation of impersonal communication in the form of cell phones most certainly doesn't help. In a recent Pew Internet report from the Family Online Safety Institute, 25 percent of teens reported being bullied or harassed on their phones; 15 percent had received a "sext"; and 34 percent admitted to texting and driving. Given such statistics, both parents and schools could ramp up education and dialogue on the physical and emotional safety issues—not to mention stress created with the use, and frequent loss, of these ubiquitous devices.

These pressures continue through college but are compounded by academic pressures and concerns about finding a job postgraduation. You might remember those stressful midterm all-nighters and worries in senior year about finding a job and paying off school loans. In fact, 85 percent of college students said they felt stressed, according to a recent poll conducted by the Associated Press and mtvU, a division of MTV Networks. About 42 percent reported feeling down, depressed, or hopeless several days in the previous two weeks. As adults, we may have had different experiences when we were in college. But our kids live in a different world, and it is our opportunity to tune in and listen to the stresses they perceive.

Stress and Relationships

If we look back to the thirteen-pronged relationship tree of Beth's family, you can just imagine how the impact of other relationships, outside the immediate family, can also add up and become potential stress triggers. Managing all of our human relationships presents a daily challenge. We all want and need different things all the time. Sometimes others want, need, and expect things from us when we're least able to provide them and the opposite holds true as well. Those are normal circumstances that already can cause high levels of stress.

But when certain relationships, particularly close, emotional ones, are threatened, or disintegrate, these moments can cause the highest levels of stress among adults and children.

The Parents' Marriage

The impact of divorce and marital strife on kids is perhaps one of the most passionately researched topics over the last two decades, especially with the high rate of divorce among Americans. I see many families before, during, and after the separation process and it can be immensely stressful on the kids. Often we use psychological methods such as talk therapy to assess and process the impact on adults and children. Recently, though scientists are developing other tools that will help us measure a person's actual stress levels biologically.

Remember that fight-or-flight skin phenomenon I mentioned earlier called the cold sweats? Researchers are now able to measure the electrical conduction in a person's skin. It doesn't hurt, and is easy to do. By using this method, scientists were actually able to show a direct association between marital conflict and children's autonomic nervous system. The researchers found lower rates of electrical conduction and more cold sweats among the children whose parents argued more, according to a 2010 study published in the *Journal of Abnormal Psychology*. The higher the rates of stress, presumably, the more cortisol there is diverting nutrients from the skin to those important muscles needed for fight or flight.

Not all separations or divorces have to be hugely stressful on kids. The point to take from this research is that strife, whether associated with divorce or not, is what makes kids stressed out. When children—just like adults—feel safe and unthreatened, they do not experience such high levels of stress and cortisol reaction. And there are plenty of studies that show that in fact, kids do much better when their parents are living separately in peace rather than living between two combatants under the same roof.

It's important to note here that, whether divorced or married, the *way* parents raise kids can be more or less stress provoking. It all depends upon their approach and behavior with their children. While it may sound obvious to some, the parent who is harsh and demanding, instead of warm and nurturing, is going to create more stress and fear in their children, unnecessarily. Many studies back up the notion that children coming from less nurturing, more stress-filled homes, are much more likely to act out at school and outside the home. These kids often have a harder time focusing, may be disciplined more frequently, and may be more likely to ignore authority figures.

Teens and Stress

If you're a parent of a teen, then you know that one of the main reasons for stressful conflict at this age is the normal desire for independence as teens mature. Parents often think that a firm approach is best. Increasingly, though, we are learning that what helps to keep kids under control, is not just ruling with the iron fist. Rather, it has to do with the level of respect within the relationship and how kids feel about their parents. In particular, in homes where there is a clear give and take of ideas, opinions, and decisions between teens and their parents, the parents may experience less conflict with their teens. In fact, in a recent Swedish study of young people's feelings and behavioral control, researchers showed that when parents cared what their kids were feeling, they were less likely to break rules.

Stress on Parents

While psychologists have been busy exploring the effects of parents' behavior on their children, much less is known about the effects of children on their parents, at least children without significant medical conditions like cancer or diabetes. You've no doubt heard the expression: "The bigger the kid, the bigger the problem." Well, this also goes for the level of stress that occurs when older kids do get out of control and misbehave. While many parents seem to think that their kids turn into aliens the moment they hit their teens, when those teens get into trouble, the level of parental stress can skyrocket. In my work with adolescents who have addiction and mental health problems, I see the devastating impact on parents. This was not the kind of stress they signed up for when they became parents. Nevertheless, by helping all family members deal with the heightened stress, most develop skills to better manage, make changes, and move forward with their lives.

Friends vs. Frenemies

It is comforting to have a few close friends with whom you can totally relax and feel social support, but most of us realize that not all friendships are created equal.

Some relationships not only cause stress, they can even threaten your cardiovascular health according to researchers at Brigham Young University. The research found that unpredictable and ambivalent friendships raise our blood pressure because they do not help us deal with stress and are themselves a source of heightened stress.

"The type of friend we are talking about is someone we may really love or care about," said Professor Juliane Holt-Lunstad, author of the 2008 study published in the *Annals of Behavioral Medicine*. "However, they can also at times be unreliable, competitive, critical or frustrating. Most people have at least a few friends, family members or co-workers that fit the bill." So, while the frenemy kind of relationship works to fuel the drama on reality TV, those may not be the healthiest of relationships to focus on in real life.

As you can see from just this basic exploration of our many, everyday stress triggers, every age presents its own unique opportunity for stress. What you can take away from reading and learning about other people's stress triggers is how different groups each experience external stress. When equipped with this information, you can relate better to, and even help alleviate, their stress, and in the process, your own.

Self-Help: The Reflective Detective

Generally speaking, we know that human beings are good at picking up what other human beings are feeling and experiencing. In recent years, scientists have identified the brain cells they believe are partially responsible for this. These specialized brain cells, called mirror neurons, will fire in the same region of your brain as they fire in the brain of another person who you may be simply observing. Often we feel like crying when we see someone else crying. Or, we get frightened during a movie when the actor looks scared. We may even get hungry watching other people eat food, even if we just ate. When it comes to stressful behavior, there is no question that being around someone who is acting stressed will stress you out, too.

Stress is very contagious. It makes sense from an evolutionary point of view that if we saw someone under stress we would worry that the same stressor would also impact us, and our mirror neurons would kick in. We still have this profound biological ability to react automatically with our ancient brain mechanisms, especially if we're not paying attention.

But we have evolved. Human beings have developed a brake to just reacting; it's a function of our prefrontal cortex. Instead of being reactive we can be reflective, and wonder about what we perceive and the resultant fight-or-flight response. I call this new skill our *Reflective Detective*. As a Reflective Detective you can look deeper into what is causing the other person's stress and whether you need to feel stressed yourself. You can reflect if you are truly in danger, and if not, reassess the situation and develop a plan of response and action.

As an example, let's look at the key moments from the scenario at the beginning of this section regarding Beth's stress attack after dinner and how things might have turned out differently had she been a Reflective Detective.

Trigger 1: Kids Not Eating

Beth could see that her kids were not eating. They were bored and so picking on each other and arguing. They didn't want to be sitting there. This meal just wasn't happening.

The Reflective Detective in her might have asked a few questions that brought Beth around to a calmer-thinking state that made her less stressed and happier:

- Did they drink their milk? (OK, they were getting nutrients.)
- Were they throwing food on the floor? (Maybe it was accidental; the kids could be expected to pick it up if they wanted a Popsicle afterward.)
- Were they tired? (We all know that tiredness and kids don't mix well and that's nobody's fault.)
- Were they just not hungry? (Entirely possible, maybe Dad gave 'em too many cheese crackers before dinner. No big deal as long it's not every single day.)
- Were they just being naughty and disrespectful? (Sometimes they were, but mostly they're good boys.)
- Had something happened at school that they didn't want to talk about, so they were creating a brilliant if annoying distraction?

Of course the best way to address the issue is to stop, look, and listen. How do you know what your kid or anyone is thinking and feeling? Ask them!

- Why weren't you hungry?
- Why did you throw food on the floor?
- What happened at school?

Take the time to stop, look, and listen. Help your kid feel as valuable as you would like to.

So step back and take a deep breath. It is most definitely a cliché, but it's a darned effective one. When we count to three or five before we allow ourselves to react emotionally, we are sending information to the thinking and rational parts of our brain. This is the part of the brain that will keep you calm, that will remind you that in the big picture, your kids are going to be fine if they don't eat chicken nuggets one night. This is the part of the brain that will allow you to be calm so you'll have a restful sleep that night. All Reflective Detectives know this trick well.

Trigger 2: Husband Not Listening

Beth felt her husband was useless and she couldn't decide who was worse—him or her kids. He couldn't control the boys and always resorted to trying to bribe them. He also never listened to her and she resented having to ask for help when what needed to be done was so obvious to her.

Here is what the Reflective Detective in her might have asked:

- Is everything going OK for him at work? (You're right, I didn't even ask.)

- Did he make dinner? (It was simple, but thank god he can cook at all.)
- What has he done to help me lately? (Actually, he took the kids on Saturday to give me a break. That was nice.)
- If we work as a team we can all relax, get the kids to bed, and then have some time together.

Do you see how Beth had many opportunities to curb her stress response and prevent it from escalating into heart palpitations, which really are not all that healthy? You, too, are capable of starting to be a Reflective Detective. Start a little at a time, and pretty soon you'll be letting your rational brain make the decisions about what to get upset over.

chapter 4

Common and Mysterious
Symptoms of Stress

Annette was a young mother of a two-month-old baby girl who showed up for her first appointment with a paralyzed right arm. Her neurologist referred her to me after he conducted every diagnostic test known to medicine, but could find nothing physically wrong. No brain tumor. No muscle tear. No problem with the nerves in Annette's arm or spinal cord. But she could not move her arm. You could throw a ball at her and she would not lift her arm to protect herself. You could poke her arm with a pencil, and she would not flinch. Her left arm appeared clinically paralyzed.

As she began to share her feelings, she told me that she loved her new baby and was devastated that she could not hold her in her arms anymore. Her mother was now caring for the infant. She was a very good grandmother. "She is probably a better mom than I could ever be," said my patient.

This was a clue. We began to explore this idea that my patient could never be as good a mom to her own daughter as her mom was to her. It was a deep-seated insecurity of which she was reminded each time the infant wriggled or her head flopped. She recalled that soon after the birth she was holding the baby and her mother snapped, "Careful, you'll drop her!"

The next day, my patient says she awoke with a paralyzed arm.

As she began to recognize that the paralysis was actually a reaction to her extreme anxiety about hurting her baby, and that she would rather sacrifice the joy than be a danger, her arm once again became fully functional. The first thing she did with it was to raise her hand and dry her freely flowing tears. At her next and last visit to me, she brought her daughter, holding her safely in her arms.

A medical mystery like this cuts right to the question of how stress and its cousin, anxiety, can manifest in both the most ordinary and most peculiar ways, and even masquerade as, or evolve into a physical illness.

While the majority of young mothers may experience an increase in anxiety when confronted with the care of a fragile newborn, most will not suffer so severely as to lose the feeling in a vital limb. The same could be said for most people and their jobs and circumstances. What is stressful for some is exciting for others. In my own field, for instance, I work with teenagers who often have psychiatric illness. To me, this job is incredible and rewarding. But many of my friends and colleagues could not imagine working with this population. "That's just too stressful," they would remark. But ask me to change the oil in my engine, and my stress level skyrockets. I would not be able to do it. So one person's stress may be another person's specialty.

But even though people perceive stressful situations differently, the body is still designed to basically respond to stress in the same way. This dichotomy is very important. On a conscious level you may not even be aware that you are under stress, especially if it becomes an unfortunate part of your daily routine. Getting on the sardine-packed subway or freeway, being unable to pay all your bills, worrying about getting a job, worrying about your weight getting out of control: All these things become familiar concerns, but never comfortable. What people need to know is that stress symptoms can affect your health *without your knowledge*. Over time, symptoms can build and plateau, build and plateau, and eventually they can begin a negative feedback loop that may affect your behavior, your feelings, and moods as well as your health.

Over the last couple of decades there has been a

greater interest among researchers on the links between stress and some of our physical symptoms. We have a much better understanding of the core physical mechanisms—the fight-or-flight response and the cortisol overload of chronic stress. According to the American Association of Stress, there are more than fifty common signs and symptoms of stress. Take a look through this list and see if you have ever experienced any of these. My hunch is that you have.

Common Signs and Symptoms of Stress

1. Frequent headaches, jaw clenching, or pain
2. Gritting, grinding teeth
3. Stuttering or stammering
4. Tremors, trembling of lips, hands
5. Neck ache, back pain, muscle spasms
6. Light-headedness, faintness, dizziness
7. Ringing, buzzing, or *popping* sounds
8. Frequent blushing, sweating
9. Cold or sweaty hands, feet
10. Dry mouth, problems swallowing
11. Frequent colds, infections, herpes sores
12. Rashes, itching, hives, goosebumps
13. Unexplained or frequent allergy attacks
14. Heartburn, stomach pain, nausea

15. Excess belching, flatulence
16. Constipation, diarrhea
17. Difficulty breathing, sighing
18. Sudden attacks of panic
19. Chest pain, palpitations
20. Frequent urination
21. Poor sexual desire or performance
22. Excess anxiety, worry, guilt, nervousness
23. Increased anger, frustration, hostility
24. Depression, frequent or wild mood swings
25. Increased or decreased appetite
26. Insomnia, nightmares, disturbing dreams
27. Difficulty concentrating, racing thoughts
28. Trouble learning new information
29. Forgetfulness, disorganization, confusion
30. Difficulty in making decisions
31. Feeling overloaded or overwhelmed
32. Frequent crying spells or suicidal thoughts
33. Feelings of loneliness or worthlessness
34. Little interest in appearance, punctuality
35. Nervous habits, fidgeting, feet tapping
36. Increased frustration, irritability, edginess
37. Overreaction to petty annoyances
38. Increased number of minor accidents
39. Obsessive or compulsive behavior
40. Reduced work efficiency or productivity
41. Lies or excuses to cover up poor work

42. Rapid or mumbled speech
43. Excessive defensiveness or suspiciousness
44. Problems in communication, sharing
45. Social withdrawal and isolation
46. Constant tiredness, weakness, fatigue
47. Frequent use of over-the-counter drugs
48. Weight gain or loss without diet
49. Increased smoking, alcohol, or drug use
50. Excessive gambling or impulse buying

It may be quite hard to believe that all of these signs and symptoms are, or have been, caused by stress. Many sound like symptoms of a real illness and disease, right? Some would send you right to the doctor in fear of a serious malady. Unfortunately, most symptoms in general are indeed nonspecific. A symptom does not always indicate its cause. Many of these symptoms sound all too familiar, while others may seem foreign, things to which you just don't relate. Some of these symptoms, such as suicidal feelings, indicate various types of mental illness. Other behaviors, like excessive gambling, may seem unimaginable.

But to discount the validity of stress symptoms, can be dangerous. It's important to listen to and observe our own behaviors and symptoms. They can very often reveal a lot about what's going on in our lives, and be the first step in managing stress.

When you understand the way we have evolved to adapt to stress, a lot of the symptoms actually start to make sense. If stress impacts the immune system, it makes sense that people under stress get more colds or seem more susceptible to allergies. If stress has an effect on the heart and blood pressure, it makes sense that people under stress get more headaches, heart disease, or have high blood pressure. If stress has an effect on your sense of well-being, can make you more depressed, or insecure, then it makes sense that people under stress may have more difficulty concentrating at work, leading them to feel inadequate or even lying to their boss about their productivity. This stress thing, at first an enormous benefit to survival, has become an incredible block to our daily moods and productivity, not to mention our broader joy and happiness.

The Stress-Insomnia Link

There are certainly a number of these symptoms that almost *everyone* can relate to. Take number 26, for instance: insomnia. There are few people I know among the general population, as well as among my patient population, who have never experienced insomnia in their lifetime. According to a recent survey published in *The American Journal of Managed Care*, almost half of respondents (46 percent) experienced some form of insomnia—whether it be difficulty going to sleep, trouble staying asleep, or insomnia so severe that it disrupts daytime activities and moods.

If you think about how this one symptom alone can affect you the next day, or the following weeks, or months if it's a bad case, you know firsthand how profoundly vulnerable we all are to stress symptoms, and how crippling one symptom of stress alone can be. While stress is not the only cause of insomnia, most experts find that when medical reasons are ruled out, sleep disturbance is most frequently caused by anxiety that people cannot manage. And what's worse is that insomnia can then in turn disrupt your life in so many ways. Sleep deficits inhibit our daytime performance, slowing down our mental capacity, making us feel more emotional, which then increases our stress even more. It becomes a vicious cycle that, left untreated, can turn into full-on anxiety and depression.

So how do you know if stress is the cause of your insomnia—or a loved one's? Sometimes the answer can be obvious when you look at the different sources of stress affecting you. For instance, starting a new job, or losing a job, can be an obvious stressor. But sometimes it's not always easy to see that stress could be the real culprit.

A good example of this is a former patient of mine who suffered from both anxiety and depression. She was a busy executive who did not have time for insomnia, nearly demanding that I prescribe sleeping pills on her first visit. Not only was she a working parent with two adolescent kids, but her identity and sense of self was intimately connected with being successful. She could not imagine herself as, in her words, "weak" and unable to manage any situation thrown her way. Indeed, she went out of her way to find those events in which she could prove herself. She believed that she thrived on stress at the office and was not bothered in the least by deadlines. Her trimly tailored suit she proudly described as her "tough skin"—a necessary ingredient for success in her male-dominated field.

What became evident after a few sessions was that home was not as manageable as work. Home was her source of malcontent, and self-doubt. Like so many people, she was cast in the almost impossible role of having to juggle these two major arenas of responsibility. As she became more comfortable in the sessions, and able to reveal her worry without fearing she would be judged (I tell my patients I'm a psychiatrist and not a judge, just for this reason), she told me her younger son was having trouble at school and she suspected he was getting involved in drugs and hanging with a bad crowd.

While she said that she could handle it, that it was part of the separation process between teen and parent, it became more and more apparent that she felt she was losing control over her preteen. Not only that, but she felt that her youngest was growing up so fast, and that she had missed a lot of his life already, and it wasn't feeling good. This person who took pride in having an answer to everything at work, was feeling increasingly inadequate at home.

What she was going through was an ongoing stress that was gnawing at her. While it was not obvious from the onset of her symptoms, she began to realize that in fact her feelings of lack of control, losing her child, and the day-to-day conflict was eating away at her and causing enough anxiety to interrupt her sleep. As she lay in her bed at night, thoughts of the day before and the day ahead would race, one after the other, relentlessly. Counting sheep was not going to solve this one.

But she was able to use her deep desire to solve problems in a positive way. Being a focused worker was a good asset, a strength she could use to help her son. She just had to find a way to first recognize the source of her stress without seeing herself as inadequate. Once she could do that she could create a plan, a creative way to get her boy back on track.

First, she delegated some of her responsibilities

at work to one of her staff. Not only did she free up some time, but her younger colleague also felt empowered, trusted by the boss to do a good job. My patient then took my suggestion to stop, look, and listen to her kid. It turned out he was also feeling stressed as he viewed himself as playing second or third fiddle to Mom's work. With this simple shift, my patient and her son, as well as some people at work, felt less stressed out and more valuable and successful. Her thoughts at night were more peaceful, less pressured, and her sleep improved without medication. She had recognized her stress, created a plan, and incorporated the help of others to get it done. Now that's what I call a "CEO of Stress."

Stress vs. Anxiety

Which comes first the chicken or the egg? We may never have a real answer to this question. Similarly, external stressors and internal responses are intricately and intimately interwoven. Stress and anxiety are closely related but they are not the same thing. If you'll recall from the last chapter, stressors are external events that require you to act.

(continued)

Depending on the stressor, you may generate a mild reaction, or a megareaction, causing the heart-pounding fight-or-flight response. A stress event can come from any situation and, depending on how susceptible you are, can result in your feeling an increase in nervousness, worry, or anger.

Anxiety on the other hand is how stress can make you feel after the initial stress event has passed. Anxiety is an internal event that may be one of several responses to an external, environmental stressor. When people say they're "stressed out," what they're really saying is that the stress outside is making them anxious inside. You may feel "stressed out" but you are really feeling *anxiety-in* from that outside stress. Stressed-out people feel ongoing worry, fear, and unease. They were unable to process and fully let go of the feelings they experienced while under direct stress. Unless you take steps to register the many stressors in daily life, those traces of stress, can grow and become harder to control. Increased anxiety then leads to confusion about how to deal with outside stressors: a perfect recipe for a variety of anxiety disorders. This is why it is so important to recognize, relax, and register the times you're experiencing a stress event, and to create a method to recover from it. Stress out? Or *get* that stress out? It's up to you.

Stress and Frustration

Everyone knows how stress-inducing feelings of frustration can be. We humans, like most animals, are designed to grab things with our hands, walk free, and express ourselves. When we have difficulty accomplishing seemingly simple things, we can easily feel frustrated. Watch a toddler try to grab a toy out of reach, or an adult waiting in a line that has a slow-moving checkout clerk. Even research on infants has shown that simple physical restraint creates a form of stress. A recent study conducted by researchers at Brigham Young University looked at patterns of distress among infants whose arms were briefly restrained. From the age of two months, the infants tried escape maneuvers and depending on who applied the restraint—a mother or a stranger such as a nurse—they were quick to vent their frustration when they couldn't move their limb.

But the insidious thing about frustration is that it feeds the stress load in a low-tech fashion. Unlike a sudden and decisive occurrence like a strike of lightning, frustration stresses the mind with a steady, low voltage. You could even call frustration the water torture of stress. Like the infamous tiny drops of water to the forehead, the first three or four are manageable. But as they continue, they are reputed to have the capacity to create great suffering. So a man at the sales desk screaming his head off is not only showing signs of stress, he has allowed his frustrated feelings to balloon into an anger response, and has become a source of stress to those around him. He did not have to let his frustration grow to such great proportions, but it is likely he just never learned to manage basic stress. And, like most people, he was unaware of how easily a few drops of frustration can quickly turn into a deep puddle of anger. Sound familiar?

Stress and Anger

Let's take another common symptom from our list, one that we see throughout our daily routines of going to the store, driving in traffic, or working at the office. It's also something we can all relate to ourselves: number 36—increased frustration, irritability, edginess, or what we all recognize as *a short fuse*. This one can be a slippery slope also, as irritability and edginess can easily turn into anger—a natural, internal emotion that can lead to dangerous external aggression for both the person experiencing it or for others in the vicinity. If you've ever seen an irate person screaming at a sales agent in an attempt to solve a basic problem, you have seen how a person can create a severe stress response in everyone around him. An outside stressor like this can indeed have a big effect on a whole bunch of people.

But what's encouraging about this phenomenon of group effect is that each of us can have a big influence in reducing that feeling of stress as well. Remember that old phrase: "If you are not part of the solution you are part of the problem?" The person who remains calm and focused in the face of an individual losing control, rather than lashing back, sends a signal to others that there is no reason to fear, or to feel stressed out. The poor behavior, and anger of a single individual can remain contained—stress to others averted.

Social Butterfly to Hermit: Stress and Depression

Stress, however, does not always lead along that straight line from frustration, to irritability to anger. Another insidious sign of stress runs in the opposite direction. Instead of culminating in anger, a person instead withdraws. They isolate themselves from people, places, and situations that can trigger stress. They develop intense anxiety and have to avoid all conflict. In order to do that, they avoid other people. Someone who was once gregarious can become a completely different person, a hermit. This person could be suffering the same amount and kind of stress as the screaming man at the customer service desk. But his way of coping with the overload is remarkably different.

To understand how someone could react in this seemingly passive way, you need only ask how many times you yourself felt like just giving up? Or how many people you know felt so beaten down they lost the will to try to solve a problem, convinced that any attempt would be fruitless? Withdrawal, or *freeze,* is the third response to danger. In the freeze mode we are hoping to become invisible so that the threat will just go away. We see this not only in human behavior, but also in nature. Scientists have found that cortisol levels in fish correlated with both learning and giving up. Fish that had higher levels of cortisol, interpreted as having more stress, did not even try to learn a maze that, if traversed, would reward them with shelter and a mate. They froze and did not even try.

When humans experience the withdrawal reaction to chronic stress, we see a context in which depression can develop. Except for a number of clinical and hereditary cases, depression does not simply happen in a vacuum. Depression can develop from the withdrawn state of mind, or what is also described as learned helplessness. Rates of depression have skyrocketed in the last decades, and much of this increase is believed to be due to unmanaged stress. An estimated 9 percent of all American adults currently suffer from depression, according to a 2010 study published in the Centers for Disease Control's latest *Morbidity and Mortality Weekly Report*. That is a very big number, as the population of the United States is over 300 million people. This means that almost 30 million of us have some form of depression. Chances are you know at least some of them, and perhaps have had a bout of depression yourself. Take a moment to reflect: How much of this depression is due to external stressors that seem overwhelming?

From an evolutionary point of view, there were times in our development when resources were sparse, danger great, and survival a daily challenge. Often it would have made sense to sequester oneself away, eat less, minimize activity to conserve energy, and stay awake at night to vigilantly ward against predators. But these responses, programmed into our DNA for generations, are overexaggerated, especially within the context of modern-day realities. Depression, then, may be one response to an external threat that is actually not at all life threatening.

The connection between stress and depression is similar to stress and anger. Chronic stress can wear you down, overwhelm you, and chip away at your resilience. If the stress has occurred because of a lost job or a personal rejection, people can more easily find themselves feeling vulnerable and powerless. Some people might even find it difficult to go about a normal daily routine. But what frequently happens is that in order to cope with stress, people choose the wrong solution. Instead of healthy lifestyle choices like exercise and healthy diet—which research has shown to help alleviate stress—people will choose to watch hours of television, smoke cigarettes, eat unhealthy foods, and drink more than normal. In essence, we may choose the freeze response to stress and hope that if we do nothing it will just pass us by. But what happens is just the opposite. This behavior reinforces the depression and a vicious cycle ensues. Think you are powerless: Make yourself powerless.

And worse, over time the depression becomes more and more entrenched as brain chemicals responsible for depression increase while those responsible for joy and pleasure decrease. In fact, the mechanism of action of most antidepressant medications is to instruct brain cells to increase the specific chemicals we know are depleted in depression. What we are also beginning to learn is how stress inhibits those cells from making the normal amount of brain chemicals to begin with. But, unfortunately, once depression has set in, the cycle of stress can be self-fueling. Researchers at Macquarie University in Sydney, Australia, recently found that teenagers who were depressed contributed to future stress in their lives because they saw life so bleakly. Because they already felt so sad, the world around them seemed sad, and full of more stress.

What you think affects how you feel is a basic law of how our brains work. Not only do we see this in people with depression, but also in people suffering from post-traumatic stress disorder (PTSD). We know that traumatic experiences may scar the psyche. But what is going on with a person with PTSD in some way actually resembles a microcosm of what happens to many people with chronic stress in general. They become unable to let go of the memories caused by a stressful event, and those traces of stress lead to anxiety with the person feeling chronically stressed out. This also makes sense from an evolutionary point of view: If we faced a life-threatening danger and escaped, it would behoove us to remember that situation and either avoid it, or respond quickly if we ever suspected it was happening again. Perhaps this deep survival mechanism explains at least some of the symptoms of PTSD including flashbacks, and an exaggerated startle response—even to the slamming of a door or the abrupt movement of another person.

But with PTSD, the stress trigger is usually a very traumatic experience. It is not seen in people who have been cut off in traffic, but rather in people who have suffered a tragic car accident. Hugely stressful events—such as rape, physical assault, accidents, natural disasters, living in a war zone or otherwise violent locale, and losing a loved one suddenly—may also trigger PTSD.

In fact, the risk of developing PTSD is higher among people with a family history of depression and anxiety. If you are someone with this type of background this is important to know, because vulnerability does not mean you have no control. The knowledge and acceptance offers you a greater opportunity to anticipate and manage your stress. This is just like someone who has diabetes running in the family and must manage their weight and calorie intake. In the case of stress and anxiety, you would need to be aware of the warning signs of stress, and have a lifelong plan to stay at least a few steps ahead of it.

Self-Help: How Do You React to Stress?

How you react to stress determines whether you'll manage it or whether it will mangle you. Now that you are beginning to build stress awareness, try to figure out some of the ways you react to stress. Go through the list of reactions at the end of this chapter. Next, think about how other people react to stress. Perhaps your spouse, or close friends. Is it different? It may well be because everyone is different. Some people seem to take everything in stride. Their naturally laid-back attitudes shine through, even in stressful situations. Another deadline?

Bring it on. The dishwasher is leaking? No problem, it'll be a simple repair. Others get anxious at the first sign of a stressful situation. Running late for a meeting? Time to panic! Stuck in a traffic jam? Let the cursing begin! Which are you? A glass half full, a glass half empty, or as Gary Larson said in one of his cartoons: "Hey! I ordered a cheeseburger."

In his own way, Gary Larson has described the four options we have evolved in response to stress. Viewing the glass as full can be seen as choosing to fight, an optimism that we will win. The pessimistic view of the glass as empty means choosing flight: We will lose. Half full or half empty represents the freeze response—paralyzed, not knowing which outcome is most likely, so better to do nothing and hope the danger passes.

But there is a fourth option that humans have evolved, a glimpse of which can be seen in "Hey! I ordered a cheeseburger." This fourth "F" is *friendship*. Although Larson does not say it directly, this cartoon presents the opportunity to solve the problem by including someone else. In a real-life situation the disgruntled customer can get his cheeseburger, but only with the help of someone else. Keep this thought, as I will come back to this in greater detail in the last chapter.

Here are some common but unhealthy reactions to stress. Do any of these describe your reactions? If you're not sure, consider keeping a "Stressor Notebook" for a week or so to monitor your reactions to stressful situations.

   Negativity: News bulletin! The world is actually not divided into those who believe the glass is half empty or half full. There is a lot of gray area in between and our stress level impacts our views about this all the time. When you're feeling overwhelmed by stress, you may automatically expect the worst or magnify the negative aspects of any situation,

   Overeating: Stress may trigger the "Cookie Monster" in all of us, tempting us to eat even when we're not hungry, and to eat the wrong thing. How often have you said to yourself, *What the heck, I'll just eat the whole bag. What difference does it make?* Or you may skip your aerobics class and lose out on a mega de-stress opportunity. Other people actually eat less under stress, prompting drastic weight loss, which isn't any better.

   Anger: How long is your fuse? Stress is what will shorten it every time. When you're under pressure, you may feel jittery, cranky, and more argumentative with coworkers, friends, or loved ones—sometimes with little provocation or about things that have nothing to do with your stressful situation. Be careful not to let loved ones become emotional punching bags for you because you couldn't find another, less harmful way to manage your stress. If you start to feel like one yourself, let your friend or loved one know that you care about them and how their stress level is leading them to hurt feelings. Chances are, they'll thank you for the reminder and your caring attitude will diffuse some of their stress and anger.

Crying: Stress may trigger crying spells: Instead of reacting to stress with anger, a tensing in the throat followed by tears that arrive seemingly without warning. Little things that are not directly related to your stress trigger may leave you in tears, such as seeing a homeless person on the street.

Depression: As you've just read in this chapter, the stress–depression link is not only common, but has been shown to chemically affect the human brain. Sometimes you might feel that your stress is so overwhelming that you can't make any decisions or don't want to see anyone. You might avoid the problem, call in sick to work, feel hopeless, or simply give up. These feelings are warning signs for chronic stress and can be a factor for developing depression and other types of anxiety disorders.

Pain: Are you taking a lot of Metamucil or Pepto Bismol for stomach discomfort? Do you ever find yourself clenching your fists or jaws? Many of us unknowingly develop muscle tension, especially in the neck and shoulders, all of which can lead to unexplained physical pain in our backs, necks, legs, not to mention headaches. What part of your body is tense right now? Is your brow furrowed? Take a moment to relax that spot, or to stretch it out.

Recognizing and understanding your stress is an important step in managing and taking back control of your life. But don't stress out about it!

part III

Stress and Your Body Systems

chapter 5

How Chronic Stress Can Harm Your Health

In the mid-1960s, the United States found itself in the midst of the Vietnam War, an invasion by The Beatles, and the Civil Rights Movement. On TV, doctors wearing white coats peddled the virtues of their favorite cigarettes. While much had been learned by this point about the science of stress hormones and what happened when the body experienced the fight-or-flight response, what was still unknown was how stressful events impacted health, or if they actually did at all. But there were a few scientists who suspected a connection.

Two such researchers were psychiatrists at the University of Washington, Drs. Thomas Holmes and Richard Rahe, who set out to create a measurement of how certain types of stress impacted peoples' health.

In a huge and unparalleled study, Holmes and Rahe surveyed about five thousand individuals on the various life events that they had experienced within the previous year. They compared these events to the current health conditions of those people. With this information, they established a classification of major life stressors, and their individual risk to health. They named these correlations *Life Change Units*. Holmes and Rahe exposed that larger Life Change Units resulted in greater risk to a person's health.

Holmes and Rahe followed up with another study among 2,500 sailors ranking stress and medical visits, which further validated their earlier findings. Later, their cross-cultural studies in Japan and Malaysia also supported the stress/illness correlation. For example, the death of a spouse appeared to have a serious impact on the surviving partner's health. In fact the survivors were ten times as likely to die within the following year than others in their age group. Similarly, spouses who divorced were twelve times as likely to get sick in the subsequent year than were married people. Those who had a score of over 300 were considered at risk for illness. Holmes and Rahe began to rank these stressors in order, assigning a Life Change Unit to each life stress. They named it the Social Readjustment Rating Scale (SRRS), more commonly known today as the Holmes and Rahe Stress Scale.

Top Ten Stressful Life Events on the Holmes and Rahe Stress Scale

Events	Life Change Units
Spouse's death	100
Divorce	73
Marriage separation	65
Jail term	63
Death of a close relative	63
Injury or illness	53
Marriage	50
Fired from job	47
Marriage reconciliation	45
Retirement	44

Now, almost 45 years later, many experts continue to refer to the Holmes–Rahe scale as a breakthrough, linking physical health directly to psychological stress and distress: the mind to the body. But the acceptance of this link between stress and illness, even in the medical community, was painfully slow. The view that the body and mind were entirely separate entities was deeply entrenched. The French philosopher René Descartes (1596–1650), who coined the phrase, "I think therefore

I am," had helped popularize the idea of dualism, a separation of mind and body. This thinking persisted for 350 years, into our own lifetime and the training of many physicians.

But the accumulating evidence, especially over the last two decades, has finally turned the tide of skepticism into wide acknowledgment of this inherent and powerful connection. In fact, an enormous number of studies have now shown that stress negatively impacts nearly every single body system, from the gut to the heart, brain to the bones, and from the muscles to the mind.

To illustrate the basic mechanisms of how stress impacts physical health I like to use a simple but brutal example—the story of the salmon. That's right, I'm talking about that pink fish from the Pacific. During the annual salmon run, the fish struggle to swim back upstream in order to spawn in the waters where they were born. It's an arduous journey back as they leap in the air, battling the currents. Their cortisol levels skyrocket, as they need every ounce of energy in the fight of their lives. But at the same time, the hormone also causes their digestion to stop and their immune systems to collapse. Once they lay their eggs, the fish are fully depleted from their journey, and they die. Harsh as it sounds, salmon are designed to undergo this evolutionary rite.

In the case of humans, however, our surges in stress

are rarely predestined in this way. Even if we are not in a life-threatening stress situation, it seems to our subconscious that we are. The brain has been wired this way for a very long time and so we experience rushes of cortisol and adrenaline on a chronic level—creating that "cortisol marinade" we discussed earlier in chapter 2.

Unlike the titanic struggle of the salmon, the sources of most of our stress are daily, psychological challenges. Nevertheless, similar damage is done to the same systems—cardiovascular, digestion, immune, as well as brain function. Stress has been found to be a culprit in aging, depression, arthritis, and diabetes. And scientists are discovering and reporting more connections between stress mechanisms and disease each year.

Stress and Heart Disease

When it comes to the huge impact stress can have on the human heart, the expression "dying of a broken heart" indeed holds an element of truth. Over the last decade, a diverse body of research from around the world has pointed to the deleterious effects of chronic stress on the cardiovascular system, and researchers continue to learn more each year. We have learned, for instance, how stress disturbs the brain and body's perception of how we should manage and metabolize food. The body breaks down food to extract energy and nutrients, but when stress hormones disrupt this process, we can develop a constellation of symptoms such as increased blood pressure, insulin resistence, too much fat around the waist, and abnormal cholesterol levels. These combined factors, commonly referred to as *metabolic syndrome,* increase the risk of heart disease, stroke, and diabetes. This syndrome is a very dangerous, but unfortunately very common condition in the United States.

A 2010 study from the University of California for instance, recently examined the correlation between psychological risk factors and the onset of the metabolic syndrome. This work confirmed what many suspected: The patients with higher levels of depression, anger expression, hostility, and pessimism had significantly higher occurrences of the metabolic syndrome.

The way stress targets the heart, and more precisely, the arteries and veins, brings us back to the story of fight and flight. During flight, the body craves energy. Energy in the body is extracted from glucose, or sugar. Insulin is the hormone that transports that sugar into the cells, where it is converted to energy. In a fight-or-flight situation, stress hormones override insulin to divert energy to where it's needed. Once the threat is gone, the body stabilizes as the stress hormones tell the body to store energy again.

When early humans had the good fortune to have excess energy, we stored it in the form of fat for those rainy days when we could not rely on getting sufficient nutrients. Fat, in this sense, is like a savings account of energy. But in a chronic stress situation, the body continually suppresses insulin because immediate energy is needed for what the brain perceives as a life-threatening situation. With less insulin available, the body has too much glucose, and more fat gets stored. All that stress is like a constant alarm signal to the body to keep storing fat, to slow down metabolism, and to increase appetite. While this was a masterful system that made sense for our ancestors' survival, those combined factors today create obesity and atherosclerosis, major causes of cardiovascular disease.

Numerous studies have shown that high cortisol can lead to an increase specifically in abdominal fat. This is the most dangerous location to have deep fat deposits as it can nearly double a person's risk of death from stroke, heart disease, or cancer. And more recent studies are shedding light (and hopefully a clue to shedding that weight) on exactly how stress may attack the arteries, even from a very young age.

In a 2011 study from the University of Buffalo, teenagers between the ages of thirteen to fifteen were asked to participate in a series of stress-inducing tasks such as reaction time, speech preparation, and ad-lib speech tasks while scientists measured their blood pressure and heart rate. What the researchers discovered was as astonishing as it was devastating. The teenagers who had higher blood pressure when asked to perform the tasks, an indicator that they were experiencing more stress, had thicker carotid arteries. The thickness of the carotid artery, the large blood vessels that guide blood from the heart to the brain, is a marker of early stage cardiovascular disease. These kids' bodies were already reacting to, and being adversely affected by stress.

What is most surprising about this research is how the effects of the stress response start so young. If the carotid arteries are already getting thick at the age of fourteen, imagine what risk those kids may face as they grow up, and how vulnerable they may be to the long-term cardiovascular effects of stress.

But it is not just in the United States where scientists are linking emotional stress with adverse consequences on cardiovascular systems. The Western diet and lifestyle have been adopted in many parts of the industrial and developing world, and with it, an increase in heart disease. Japanese researchers recently collected and analyzed data in a large-scale study called the Circulatory Risk in Communities Study (CIRCS). The scientists

"You're Making My Hair Gray!"

A lot of parents blame the stress from their kids for turning their hair white or gray. "I'm pulling out my hair because of you!" I heard one parent say to their kid. "Not the gray ones!" the kid shot back. Stress seems to be the cause of so many other disorders and diseases these days. Isn't it just common sense that stress would be responsible for these first, upsetting signs of aging? In fact, stress has been suspected as the trigger of conditions such as *alopecia areata* (hair loss), *telogen effluvium* (scalp disorder that leads to hair loss), and, in rare cases, pigmented hair loss (when just the darker patches fall out). Also, gray hair has been seen as a symptom of various illnesses such as thyroid disease, fibromyalgia, and vitamin B12 deficiency. But exactly why someone's hair pigment changes and when, is still, by and large, a great mystery. If you think about it, a strand of hair can't change color once it has already grown in, unless it has been dyed of course. Typically, half the population will have hair that is 50 percent gray by the age of fifty, according to dermatologists. Given that many people just happen to be raising teenagers at the same time as hair pigments start to change in most people, I can see that this myth will stay around for a long time to come.

rated 6,929 men and women for anger and stress-related tension while 901 men and women rated themselves for depression. What was disturbing was that men who scored high on *anger-in,* or suppressed anger, actually had a greater chance of increased blood pressure, known to be a leading cause of heart disease and stroke. People with depression did not do that much better, with twice the risk of a stroke, and seven times the risk for coronary heart disease. This research further supports the notion that letting out your anger in a healthy way is probably better for your heart health than trying to ignore or suppress it. That this major study comes out of Japan has other significance. It is not just the American medical community that is now recognizing this critical mind-body connection. As I say to my patients, it's not your anger that will get you in trouble. It's what you do with it that can get you in trouble. Or, in fact, what you don't do with it.

Stress and the Gut

From the time we are children we describe our experience of nervousness and unease by saying we have "butterflies" in the stomach. Our guts, it sometimes seems, form an early mental repository for feelings of fear and stress. Some folks lose their appetites completely when upset and stressed out, while others go in the opposite direction and consume tons of needless sweets and fat-laden calories. Either way, gastrointestinal disorders may affect up to 70 percent of people at some point in life, women more often than men. Oddly enough, these aches and gurgles of the gut are not usually from any diagnosable physical malady, such as infection or disease. That news, however, won't help all those people experiencing very real pain, bloating, and discomfort.

While a regular diet of donuts and fried clams may be a frequent culprit in many cases of gastrointestinal discomfort, the chronic kind of GI disorders we're discussing here won't get better with a few Rolaids. You or someone you know, have unfortunately experienced one of these many functional gastrointestinal disorders: irritable bowel syndrome, chronic constipation or its opposite, acid reflux, GERD, as well as various other digestive disorders common among both children and adults.

While multiple factors can contribute to the development of one of these GI disorders, numerous studies do show that stress is a frequent trigger of symptoms. A recent Swiss study, for instance, measured the prevalence of GI disorders in a sample of 668 healthy men and women while also taking into account their levels of stress—2 out of every 3 reported at least one GI disorder. With chronic stress the symptoms increased significantly. This research is powerful evidence suggesting that in order to ease the stomach, it helps to ease the stress.

The world around us has to be navigated in order to get food, one of the basic requirements of living. It makes evolutionary sense that we have evolved an elegant and complex communication between our brains and our *gastro* (stomach) *intestinal* (the small and large intestines), or GI, tract. As nature is fiscally conservative, it would also make sense that many of the same chemicals that transmit messages in the brain would be used to communicate with the GI tract. This is indeed the case and happens automatically as the *enteric* (gut) nervous system uses hormones such as serotonin to communicate and interact with the central nervous system and brain. Think about what happens with everyday digestion. When food is consumed and has entered the gut, special cells lining the digestive tract tell muscle cells to initiate a series of intestinal movements that push food along, breaking it down into nutrients. When a certain amount of food is consumed, and nutrients extracted, a signal is sent back to the brain. Most people simply know when they've had enough to eat. That is your enteric nervous system at work. Scientists often describe this phenomenon as the *brain gut axis*.

The interconnection between the brain and gut

creates a pathway between *environmental* (external) or *psychological* (internal) stress and GI distress. We've all had the experience of heartburn, diarrhea, constipation, and stomachaches. Remember how often kids complain of stomach pain before school, or on the day of a test? Stress can trigger and inflame gastrointestinal pain and other symptoms. But at the same time GI distress itself can frequently trigger more psychological stress. As part of the fight-or-flight response digestion stops or slows so that the body can reroute all internal resources to confronting a perceived threat. After danger has passed, the brain sends a message to the enteric nervous system to help regulate digestion once again.

But with the chronic stress so many people experience, the message to the gut may get delayed, or never even get sent. Not turning off the fight-or-flight response can lead to difficulty digesting food, and increasing the need to use the bathroom a lot more. This can be embarrassing for most people, and just lead to more stress about whether or not your gut will betray you in social situations.

In fact, gastrointestinal disorders and their connection to stress are so ubiquitous that a cohort of UCLA physicians recently created a professional framework for treating patients suffering from this tricky cycle. Their paper, published in *The American Journal of Gastroenterology* in 2011, laid out suggestions for physicians who care for patients with GI disorders to also screen for psychological experiences such as anxiety, fear of accidents, depression, and even suicidal thoughts.

These guidelines are a major step forward in helping treat people with GI tract disorders. While the most successful therapies for GI tract problems combine both medication and a program for stress relief, in some cases medication is not necessary at all. Our brains turned on the fight-or-flight response, and our brains can turn it off with the right training. We will get to some of these mental techniques later in this book.

Stress and the Immune System

Your immune system is like a protective internal army that fights off foreign biologic invaders when they attack. Comprised of specialized teams of white blood cells, this delicate architecture also has a fierce ability to keep us healthy. Sometimes you get a sore throat, a minor canker sore, or a fatigue headache. You feel the onset of a cold or flu, but trust that within a few days your body's immune system will kick it and you'll feel better. This is the normal, healthy body at work.

Stress impairs the immune system, leaving us more vulnerable to infection. It can also accelerate infection

while slowing down the healing process. Even a decade ago, research among HIV-infected men showed
that those with higher rates of stress and less social
support experienced a more rapid progression of AIDS.
More recently, scientists from Ohio State investigating
how long it takes for a wound to heal, found that those
with more stress heal more slowly.

Scientists agree that long-term, chronic stress increases exposure to cortisol, which can damage the immune system. How this destructive mechanism works
is an active and exciting area of research. A group of
scientists from the David Geffen School of Medicine at
UCLA, led by immunologist Dr. Rita Effros, are studying the white blood cells of caregivers of patients
with Alzheimer's, and mothers caring for chronically
ill children. What the researchers have discovered
is the white blood cells of those individuals under
chronic stress do not behave normally. With the high
levels of cortisol present, they are unable to reproduce
quickly and efficiently. This same cortisol-influenced
occurrence in cell activity has also been associated
with diseases including osteoporosis, HIV, and heart
disease.

There are of course many reasons and ways in which
we humans contract disease. Despite great progress, we
will never have complete control over these factors.
New viruses arise from different parts of the globe and

bacteria will always be with us. But we have evolved a way to fight these microscopic dangers: our immune system. However, it is up to us to keep it in good working order. Managing your stress is more likely to boost your immune system than over-the-counter vitamins and supplements, and is a resource that will never run out once you know how to do it.

Stress and the Brain

By now you have a good idea of how our body can be adversely affected when stress becomes chronic and the stress response—fight, flight, or freeze—remains active. As each year goes by, technology improves and scientists are finding more ways to unravel the mystery of stress on the body. One of the most exciting areas of research currently offering great promise for helping people to help themselves, is the study of how stress impacts the brain.

It has been known for many years that stress adversely affects the mammalian brain. Researchers first started observing the impact of acute stress on the brains of World War II pilots. Even pilots who performed extremely well during training could crash their planes in battle. Why? Thinking errors caused by battlefield stress. Over the following decades, researchers have continued to find more and more correlations between chronic stress and brain performance.

Recently, various research groups have shown that stress may especially impact brain functions like memory, behavior, and reasoning abilities. Using a classic method of induced stress called the Trier Social Stress Test (TSST), in which subjects are stressed by a public speaking exercise, Ohio University psychiatrists recently measured performance differences between individuals under stress and nonstress conditions. As you probably anticipated, participants who experienced stress had more difficulty with tasks requiring intellectual performance, problem solving, and memory. Those who did not feel stress, as measured by the TSST, performed the same tasks more effectively.

Animal and human research consistently reveal that the stress hormones cortisol, and in some cases adrenaline, can change the very architecture of the brain, in turn affecting our abilities and our behavior. Interestingly, the main targets of stress hormones are not the brain areas we rely on for basic functions such as breathing and digestion, but the areas of the brain that make human beings, well, human. One of these areas is the prefrontal cortex (PFC). It is in our PFC where we decide who is a threat, decide how to respond to danger, and develop a plan of rational reaction to stressful events. From within our PFC we choose to be trusting, benevolent, and sympathetic toward others. But when this ability is inhibited and our rational response is compromised, the resulting symptoms can be anxiety, depression, more fear, and more stress.

As with most of the brain, even large areas with specific functions are divided, subdivided, and even sub-subdivided into areas of specialty. The PFC is no different. Scientists have been able to distinguish that the back, or dorsal (like the dorsal fin of a shark) part of the PFC has a slightly different function than the front or ventral part, and that the medial part, toward the middle, is different than the lateral part, toward the sides. For scientists, researchers, psychiatrists, neurologists, and other specialists these are extremely important distinctions. For example, the dorsomedial prefrontal cortex has a different specificity than the posterior dorsolateral location. But in general, for the purposes of this book, the prefrontal cortex will be addressed more globally, with the understanding that the general function of the PFC remains: to integrate complex information into making decisions, the locus of morality, and perhaps even the site of personality.

But when it comes to the PFC, there is good news. Damage caused by chronic stress appears, in many cases, to be reversible. Exciting studies on brain plasticity are multiplying and being replicated each year.

Recently, University of Oregon researchers recruited two groups of students for a series of MRI brain scans. One group were medical students who were preparing for a major exam, the other group were not under any psychological duress. During the scans, students performed mental tasks that required them to shift attention between the color and action of various objects. The MRI studies confirmed that the medical students' abilities were impaired compared to the control group. But a month after the exams, the same two groups of students underwent the same tasks. This time, the medical students performed equally well. These persuasive results suggest that the impact of short-term stress to the PFC is temporary. Other brain findings however, may be more insidious: Individuals who are subjected to severe stress or trauma, or children who grow up under long-term stressful conditions, suffer changes to brain structures and functions that appear more difficult to restore.

The implications of this kind of research are profound: with proper interventions to reduce stress, many people could protect and improve brain functions. But that possibility is not isolated to the brain. Stress reduction helps maintain all body systems. Heart disease would be less frequent, obesity may fade, and our immune response would be more able to fight disease. Our brains, the regulator of all, would be able to think more clearly, learn more efficiently, and perpetuate a cycle that continues to decrease stress. We will all experience stress of varying degrees throughout our days and lives. How it impacts our bodies depends on how we choose to manage it.

part IV

Addressing Your Stress

chapter 6

Healthy Responses to Stress

When Martha opened her cousin's wedding invitation it made her happy for about thirty seconds. Soon after she read the details, she started to feel peeved. She would have to buy a dress, and was reminded that she could no longer fit into any of her old ones. She convinced herself it wasn't worth losing weight unless it was her own wedding, but then that was unlikely to ever happen. She hadn't had a date in over a year. On this topic, she would get a painful earful, as always, from Aunt Claire. The thought of asking her boss for the extra day off to travel concerned her as she barely survived the last set of layoffs. And how was she going to afford the trip and a gift? She already had a huge credit card bill. This wedding was really the last thing she could deal with at the moment. How was she going to get out of it?

Like Martha, I think we've all had moments when

things that should make us happy do just the opposite. It doesn't take a big negative event to set off a bunch of stress triggers in our lives. Indeed, big and scary things rarely occur with great frequency. And yet we all have our tipping point, when we go from a delicate balance to a scale whose cross bar goes up with the added weight on your shoulders. So even a positive event, like a wedding, that comes at the wrong time can set off a cascade of stressful feelings about a whole range of issues completely unrelated to the event. For Martha, this invitation caught her not only at a bad time, but also in the wrong frame of mind.

She was struggling with a weight problem. She was unhappily single and was always chastised about that by relatives who are supposed to care. She was having some financial problems she didn't want to compound, and was concerned about her job security. All of these triggers were set off within seconds of opening an invitation for a supposedly happy event.

Identifying Stress Responses

The chronic stress that Martha was already experiencing, which she may not have been aware of, led her to do what we all do when we're not on the alert for stress triggers: Open the gate to automatic negative thoughts. *I'm so fat, my cousin will be embarrassed by me. With this butt, I won't look good in anything. Aunt Claire's right, I won't ever meet anyone. I'm sure I'll lose my job if I ask for a day off.* These are all negative and unproductive thoughts that have nothing to do with reality.

Such thoughts increase negative feelings like fear, anxiety, and low self-esteem. They are self-defeating and critical, even vicious. But you can't seem to shut them off. They just pop up over and over and make you feel worse and worse. Automatic negative thinking is one of the most unhealthy and destructive responses to stress.

Remember, how you respond to stress triggers is crucial toward managing the amount and the impact of stress in your life. Ordinarily, receiving a wedding invitation should not be a source of stress. But critical thoughts creep up even on people who think they have things under control because of the insidious way that chronic stress works on us. As you'll recall, it is not usually the big stress events that lead to chronic stress, but rather the generous and regular helpings of smaller stress triggers of modern life that set off our hardwired and overactive stress reactions. When we have chronic stress and feel anxious, the risk for negative automatic thinking increases. And when we experience this thinking, it in turn increases our anxiety. This state of mind can lead us in all kinds of directions—to depression, to anger, and in some extreme cases, even to violence toward oneself or others. It's as if stress has turned your mind into some kind of never-ending roller-coaster ride.

But humans have a powerful built-in mechanism for counteracting this cycle and for modifying stress in general. The engine for this system is in your prefrontal cortex (PFC), which I mentioned in the last chapter. The PFC, located right above your eyeballs, is the most evolved part of the brain and the center of rational thought, empathy, and planning. More than any other part of our bodies, the PFC is what makes us rational beings. Your PFC is a hidden resource that, if used and trained like a muscle, can enable you to counter the negative thinking that feeds, and feeds off of, the chronic stress you or a loved one may be experiencing throughout your daily life.

What you think influences what you feel. But what you think is based on what you perceive. To manage stress you have to shift your brain from that *feeling* state, back to the *thinking* state. You first have to recognize that you have perceived a stressor and then decide what to do about it. The acts of perception, analysis, and decision making happen in your PFC.

The PFC Shift

To understand how to tap into the strength of your PFC, let's recap briefly what stress triggers do to us. Whether a lion charges, or someone suddenly cuts us off in traffic, the same thing happens. Our internal fight-or-flight-or-freeze mechanism snaps on and, without thinking, we react. If we don't run, climb a tree, or swerve out of the way, we may increase our risk for injury or becoming someone's lunch. As you'll recall, your HPA axis kicks into gear flooding your body with the stress hormones adrenaline and cortisol. Under normal circumstances, the body is designed to reregulate on a hormonal level. But with the persistent and chronic stress triggers so many of us experience over time, the reregulation process is disrupted. This subsequent chemical wear and tear on the body can lead to a variety of issues and illnesses, as you learned in the last chapter.

So how can we change the course of chronic stress in our lives? The simple answer is: Use our brains. More specifically, that means to use our PFC. For the most part, we use the different regions of our brains unconsciously. When we're being creative, problem solving, and reasoning with others, we are using our PFC. Some people call the PFC our "executive center" or "brain CEO" because this area plays the greatest role in our decision-making processes as well as filtering the often overwhelming emotions sent by our limbic systems.

When we experience intense emotions like anger that can lead us to lose control and act out, we are indeed being directed by the amygdala or *limbic* section of the brain—the primitive region nearer to the base of the skull that is activated for our very basic survival. Millions of years old, this region is also activated during our experiences of fight, flight, or freeze. Yet, we are completely unaware of it, especially as many stress triggers seem so normal in everyday life. How often do you sense feelings of high emotions, fear, anger, even physical symptoms like a racing heartbeat, when someone rudely blabs on a cell phone next to you, or when you're treated disrespectfully by a store clerk, or when you're stuck behind a car going slower than you want to? Think about it. Have you ever kicked a vending machine? Cursed at another driver? Or maybe broken down in tears because you ran out of detergent and you really wanted to wear that purple dress the next day? This is your limbic brain at work.

By contrast, if you can recognize what you are feeling and why, then stop to process an emotion—such as aggravation over a frozen-up computer screen—you are using your PFC to modify your entire physiological reaction to this stress trigger. This very tiny action can mean the difference between someone trying to calmly problem solve, or possibly escalating to an irrational action like punching the computer. Things like that might be funny in a movie because we all relate to the same frustrations. But we've also all experienced the occasional angry rants by other people in real life, which don't make us laugh. Instead, we tend to find the behavior of that person to be childish and ridiculous, or even scary.

Another key reason to learn to shift from limbic responses to the PFC is the power of anger and fear as stress triggers, and the impact it has on your body. Allowing fears, anxiety, and worries to run amok breeds only more stress. A striking example of this was shown in a recent study of women and the fear of breast cancer. Researchers at Beth Israel Deaconess Medical Center in Boston looked at the levels of stress experienced by women waiting for a breast cancer diagnosis. Over a five-day period, saliva samples from 126 women undergoing breast biopsies were collected in order to measure their levels of stress hormones. The researchers found that cortisol levels in the 73 patients who found out they needed further testing were comparable to those in the 16 patients who learned they really had breast cancer. Understandably, both groups had higher cortisol levels than the 37 patients who found out their biopsy results were benign. What this indicates is that simply the anxiety experience felt by those who needed further testing raised their stress to the same levels of women who learned they actually had cancer.

A possible cancer diagnosis is frightening, but as frightening as getting an actual cancer diagnosis? Apparently so. When we are afraid, overtired, or under intense emotional or physical stress, we reflexively bypass the PFC's higher-functioning capacity. We imagine worst-case scenarios, we run angry dialogues in our minds, and devolve emotionally. In children, such behaviors are called tantrums. At least toddlers have an excuse for screaming and crying on the supermarket floor—a not yet fully formed PFC. Researchers believe the PFC is fully formed by the age of twenty. When adults lose control, I call it *going limbic*. The solution to this problem? Keep it in the PFC. As I say to my patients, staff, colleagues, and anyone who will listen: Don't go limbic: Keep it frontal.

The study looking at women with the potential diagnosis of cancer reveals an important component of our human brain. Even the *anticipation* of a future filled with fear is enough to have a powerful effect. This is a critical insight: We really do have powerful brains. And if thinking can increase our stress levels and anxiety in a negative way, then we can use and train the same brain to move us in an opposite direction.

Your PFC "IQ"

How proficient are you at using your PFC? Let's take a short quiz and see how you score. Select the response that most closely matches what you actually do, and not what you want to do. What you feel and what you do are usually going to be quite different.

1. Your friendly and nice neighbor is having a loud party and you have to get up the next day for work. You:
   a. Call the police.
   b. Scream "TURN IT DOWN!" out the window.
   c. Call or go over to ask if they can turn down the music.
   d. Join the party and be sleepy at work but still productive.
2. After an exhausting day you come home and your husband and kids look at you and ask, "What's for dinner?" You:
   a. Lecture them on how they're all spoiled and ungrateful.
   b. Ignore them.
   c. Calmly respond, "I don't know, let's figure it out together."
   d. Use it as an excuse for all of you to go to a restaurant.
3. The cable service stopped working for the third time in a month. You call and:
   a. Tell off the customer service rep.
   b. Demand to speak to a supervisor.
   c. Calmly explain the situation and frustration this has caused and make a follow-up plan.
   d. Start reading that book you've been ignoring.

Those who picked A most of the time are likely to have experienced the most stress in these situations. Though we may be tempted to choose the A response because these problems are frustrating, most of us know on a certain level that A is not the most productive, nor the healthiest response. For those who picked B or C, you fall into an average range of responses that people experience. You experience some stress over these situations, and if you're tired or feeling anxiety already, might be tempted to choose A. Be aware of this possible survival slip which leaves you vulnerable to being directed by your limbic system and not your PFC. When you go with your brain CEO, you are actually decreasing stress.

What we really aim for here is to get to the D response as often as possible. Some people may think that D is the *weak* response, that you're not getting things done, unless you choose an A response. But you are just as likely to get things done with a D response and at a much lower stress cost to yourself and those around you.

The D responses epitomize the great phrase: "When life deals you lemons make lemonade." In every situation there is the potential for a creative response. Having a calmer brain allows you to access those creative resources. In psychiatry we have a term for this: sublimation. This wonderfully adaptive and emotionally mature human response takes feelings that could be *de*structive and turns them into something *produc-*

tive. While sublimation was originally described as an unconscious process, there is no reason why this cannot be perfectly conscious and volitional. Lemons or lemonade becomes a *choice* and a choice shifts the locus of stress from something out of your control (which will always leave you more stressed and anxious), to taking control (which allows you to be involved in the solution to whatever degree you decide). This is what we can do with our PFC: assess the problem, find solutions, and anticipate the outcome of those decisions.

Learning to use your PFC requires practice. Our limbic system and the emotions we experience are powerful. By learning to regulate our reactions, we are not becoming robotic, we are acting to reduce stress. Many people might assume this ability is something that will automatically come with age, like wisdom. But I know many an unwise adult and a number who have been bogged down with worry, anxiety, and many health problems until the very end. You can learn to use your PFC at any age, and the sooner the better, if you really want to diminish stress in your life.

part V

Managing Your Stress

chapter 7

Lifestyle Balance to Minimize Stress

Always a force of calm in her children's and friend's lives, Elaine lost her lifelong emotional balance about a year after she lost her husband. As her youngest headed off to college, she began to feel fearful, lonely, and anxious for what seemed the first time in her life. She lost weight, stopped cooking, and rarely left the house. When Elaine's daughter June came home to visit she could see the toll that stress had taken on her mom. At college, June had started to meditate as a way to manage the stress of her courses. She thought her mom could also benefit from the relaxation and improved concentration she'd discovered. Together they came up with several small lifestyle changes. These included taking twenty minutes for a daily walk or meditation session, making daily calls to one of her children, trying new recipes, and joining a garden club. At first Elaine was skeptical. It seemed a little unconventional, especially the meditation. But with encouragement from her kids, Elaine went on the plan. Within two months, she felt as if she had shed a skin and rediscovered her formerly calm and strong self.

Elaine was able to reclaim her sense of equilibrium. Her stress hadn't quite taken over her health to such a degree that medical treatment was necessary. And while I am biased and believe that most people can benefit from psychotherapy, sometimes it is impractical and even unavailable. But it did take an intervention of sorts and one Elaine must have known she needed, as she was willing to give it a try. The small adjustments in her life required only some discipline, some time, and some belief that it might work. While the suggestions seemed simple, in fact each of the adjustments she incorporated into her life has current scientific evidence supporting their efficacy in relieving chronic stress. All together, they brought her back to a more relaxed and balanced state of mind and a place where she could start to enjoy her life again.

Mind-Body Stress Interventions

Forty years ago, the term *mind-body medicine* was virtually unknown, and what was known of the concept had no bearing in the world of "real" medicine. At that time, Dr. Herbert Benson was just starting a medical practice as a young cardiologist, and he began to notice that when his patients came in for checkups, many became nervous and the experience would elevate blood pressure levels. Benson had a hunch that it might be the stress of the visit itself that caused a change in the body's response. This view, however, ran quite contrary to the medical literature of the day.

But eventually, Benson decided to test out his theory that it was stress that caused the elevated blood pressure, or hypertension. He returned to Harvard Medical School, his alma mater, to set up some experiments that would allow him to measure and observe the impact of stress. In his early research, he and his team worked with squirrel monkeys, and observed that in fact high blood pressure was related to voluntary behaviors.

But the studies that created momentum within the medical community to accept a mind/body connection, and how our minds could possibly even *control* what was going on in our bodies, were Benson's research on practitioners of Transcendental Meditation. Benson himself wasn't sure he wanted to embark on this study, as it seemed on the fringe of mainstream medicine but what he observed would begin to change the medical perception of the mind's impact on the body.

All the subjects had healthy and lower than average blood pressures levels, and they themselves believed it was the result of their meditation practice. Benson's team first measured the subjects' regular resting blood pressure, metabolism, heart rate, brain waves, and rate of breathing. Then, they took the same measurements after the subjects had meditated for twenty minutes. The difference was impressive. By merely altering thought patterns, each individual experienced decreases in their metabolism, rate of breathing and heart rate, and had slower brain waves. These responses were the very opposite of the fight-or-flight-or-freeze stress response and opened a door to understanding how deep, focused meditation impacted physiological mechanisms. It was Dr. Benson who named it the *relaxation response*.

The Relaxation Response

While acceptance within the medical establishment has taken several decades to percolate, the relaxation response is now viewed as a powerful innate resource we humans have in our arsenal for combating chronic stress. Subsequent studies over the last several decades have shown that the relaxation response may not only reduce stress when practiced routinely, but can lower blood pressure and possibly reduce heart disease rates, help manage weight, reduce pain and asthma symptoms, as well as relieve anxiety, and lift some types of depression. While it is not viewed as a total replacement of medication, current research suggests the relaxation response is worth trying, especially in patients with hypertension. In a recent study at Massachusetts General Hospital, researchers conducted a double blind, randomized trial of 122 patients with hypertension, ages fifty-five and older. Half were given relaxation response training and the other half received information about blood pressure control. After eight weeks, 34 of the patients who practiced the relaxation response, slightly more than half, were able to reduce their resting blood pressure to the point where they could enter the study's second phase, in which they could try to reduce the levels of their blood pressure medication. During that second phase, 50 percent were able to eliminate at least one blood pressure medication. In the control group who were not utilizing the relaxation response, only 19 percent were able to eliminate their medication.

This was just one of the dozens of studies on the relaxation response to conclude that it can indeed modify the chronic stress cycle by helping the body's parasympathetic nervous system reregulate stress hormones. It is believed that one of the ways we do this is by the body's own creation of higher levels of nitrous oxide gas. If that sounds vaguely familiar, it could be that you've been to the dentist recently and had a dose of nitrous oxide, also known as laughing gas, that both relaxes the smooth muscle tissue in the arteries and aids blood flow. The body naturally manufactures more nitrous oxide gas when it is deeply relaxed.

Considering that the tremendous benefit of such a practice is right at our PFC, and doesn't cost anything, it is surprising that so many people are still unaware of it. But physicians don't routinely learn the relaxation response in medical school, and mainstream, modern culture is not always interested in slowing down. If anything, it's unfortunately the opposite—the quick fix—that many people demand. But if you think regular meditation could fit into your lifestyle, some simple instructions are provided at the end of this chapter. In addition to meditation, there are also many ways that you can achieve the relaxation response and combat your chronic stress.

Stop and Smell the . . . Mango?

We've all heard the phrase, "Stop and smell the roses," to get you to slow down and enjoy life. Indeed, that's one way to keep stress at bay. But when it comes to scents that can seriously decrease stress, skip the roses and grab a lemon, a mango, or some lavender. These fragrant plants have been found to contain *linalool*, a naturally occurring chemical in many flowers and spice plants. For the first time, Japanese researchers have shown that inhaling certain fragrances can actually change gene activity and blood chemistry in ways that reduce stress. In the lab, scientists exposed rats to stressful conditions and measured immune system cellular activity. While under stress, some of the rats inhaled linalool and the others did not. In those exposed to linalool, stress levels returned to normal. The scientists also observed that the inhalation of linalool reduced activity in more than a hundred genes known to become overactive when stressed. These findings could one day lead to customizable, gene-targeted stress-relief products, giving new meaning to the idea of "aromatherapy."

Exercise for a Healthy Mind

Human beings were designed for physical activity.
What we have seen in the last half century has been an
increase in sedentary behavior, especially in car cultures, where humans drive to do errands or go to work,
and where a great many of us then proceed to sit frozen
in front of a computer all day. Sedentary lifestyles are a
breeding ground for stress, anxiety, and, increasingly,
depression. While it has become almost a cliché to say
that exercise makes you feel better, and I remind my
patients of this all the time, it couldn't be more vitally
true. Regular exercise can help relieve chronic muscle
tension and pain. It also helps fight fatigue, indigestion,
and insomnia caused by the buildup of daily triggers.

Not only this, but exercise is one of the most effective ways to combat anxiety and depression caused by
chronic stress. A focused activity, like aerobics or cy-
cling helps take your mind off of the problems of your
day as well as minimize any negative thinking that
may arise. Some people prefer strenuous exercise in order to burn calories. But for stress reduction, a simple
twenty-minute daily stroll can clear your mind, give
you perspective, and ease stress. The more we learn
about the benefits of exercise, the more it is viewed as
critical for keeping your body *and* your mind strong and
resilient.

One recent study published in the journal *Psycho-somatic Medicine* showed that in some people exercise may even be as effective as antidepressants. In the research, 202 subjects with major depression were randomly assigned a home exercise program, the anti-depressant Zoloft, or a combination of exercise and medication. After four months, those who exercised had similar improvement levels as those who had been assigned the medication. More important, ten months later people who exercised had fewer relapses into depression than those who had stayed on medication for only four months, and even less relapse in people who had voluntarily continued to exercise during that time. If exercise can be this effective with depression, you can be sure it will have an impact on counteracting other effects of stress.

Why and how exactly does this happen? Scientists have found that part of the reason is neurochemical. Exercise actually reduces levels of adrenaline and cortisol—those stress hormones that you'll recall are useful in fight, flight, or freeze—but can be harmful when your body doesn't need them. Exercise also stimulates the production of endorphins, which are brain chemicals that act as both natural pain relievers and mood enhancers. You've heard of the term, *runner's high,* right? Those are endorphins. You don't have to run to produce them; any type of exercise will do the job.

Afterward, you are rewarded with feelings of relaxation, confidence, and very often a positive attitude. It is this reward that reinforces the runner's desire to go out and run the next day.

But exercise also has compound effects that counterbalance stress. When you commit to an exercise program you begin to see changes that can have a profound effect on your psyche. As you lose weight and get in shape, you feel better about yourself. You gain strength, stamina, and increase your energy level. Your confidence increases as your anxieties quiet down. The physical symptoms of stress you may have adapted to, like tensed muscles, clenched jaw or tightened facial expressions, neck pain, diarrhea, rapid heart beating, and a short fuse, to name just a few, will gradually melt away as you lower your overall chronic stress levels. Ultimately, you are exercising to achieve relaxation.

So when Elaine began her daily walks, alternating with meditation on days she couldn't get out, she was lowering the levels of unnecessary stress hormones in her body at the same time as she was increasing her natural energy. But there was another important part of the plan that also helped Elaine—the gardening club. The weekly gathering of like-minded peers created a new social network for Elaine. She became good friends with several of the members and couldn't understand why she hadn't joined years ago. It turns out that social relationships are some of the best antistress treatments available. The fourth option to fight, flight, or freeze: friendship.

Your Social Network

Our connections with other people make us happy. Humans are social creatures and when we are spending time with our family, our friends, neighbors, or community members, we are meeting a fundamental and biological need—being part of a group. When we're socializing we're exchanging ideas, we're listening to each other, making each other feel valued and respected, affirming our place in the group. We offer help and we receive help. On a deep evolutionary level, these seemingly ordinary motions are vitally important to both our mental and physical health, even to our longevity. So a truly effective stress-reduction plan is definitely going to include socializing.

When it comes to alleviating stress though, random socializing isn't what works best. It appears that quality over quantity is a major factor in the social connection you make. Research has shown that middle-aged women in happy marriages or close partner relationships had a lower risk for cardiovascular disease when compared with those in less satisfying relationships. Many other studies have shown that individuals who enjoy healthy and satisfying relationships with friends, family, or a significant other are simply happier. Generally speaking, the happier you are, the better you can weather stressful situations knowing you have a strong support network to lean on. Likewise, these people have fewer health problems overall.

Meanwhile, there is equally compelling research that has linked poor interactions with family and friends with inferior health. A lack of social ties has been associated with depression, dementia, and an increase in mortality. Not having meaningful attachments and social interaction has even been called a risk factor for death. In a meta-analysis of 148 long-term studies, which included more than 300,000 people, Brigham Young researchers found that individuals who lacked strong relationships had a 50 percent increased risk for premature death when compared with those with strong relationships. This is greater than the risk of obesity and physical inactivity, and the same as someone who smokes fifteen cigarettes a day. Human beings need to be around other human beings.

In a way, this seems like common sense. When people have strong emotional ties, they can more easily get help when dealing with stress or times of crisis. Your support network is there to listen and give you helpful advice. Family members and friends may also help guide you toward staying calm, making healthy decisions, and encouraging you to seek health care if necessary. But scientists are also looking at other biological reasons why emotional bonds protect us from stress. Neuroscientists are studying the impact of hormones such as oxytocin, nicknamed the "bonding" or "cuddle" hormone that are produced in the brain during certain types of human interactions. Studies with mothers of young babies, for instance, found increases in oxytocin levels when the mothers were holding or near their babies.

There is even current research studying what happens when oxytocin is randomly administered to various people. In one study, Swiss scientists found that couples that sprayed an aerosol of oxytocin into their noses were able to resolve conflicts better. At the same time, their cortisol levels decreased, suggesting that they were less stressed, less angry, and more socially connected. So the bottom line is that your strong relationships, whether you are giving or receiving, provide you with an inexpensive and simple way to alleviate stress. Naturally, our relationships fluctuate throughout our lives, but it is important to nurture and appreciate our friends, family, and close social connections. These interactions not only provide a strong buffer against chronic stress, but make us happier overall. Perhaps this is not confined to *strong* social connections

but to *any* social connection. Any connection to another person has the potential to reduce stress, an idea
we will explore in the last chapter.

It would be wonderful if there were a way to avoid
every source of stress we encounter in our daily lives.
But that would be impossible. What you can do is practice your innate abilities to combat stress. This includes
working on developing your PFC reaction to stress triggers, as well as by learning how to activate your relaxation response. These techniques can help you achieve
equilibrium in your emotions and a habit of emotional
balance. With practice, you will undergo a physiologic
shift that enables you to counter the stress reaction before you become overwhelmed by it.

How to Awaken Your Relaxation Response

Specialists at the Benson-Henry Institute for Mind
Body Medicine at Massachusetts General Hospital say
that the relaxation response can be elicited by a variety
of meditative techniques including diaphragmatic
breathing and repetitive prayer such as chanting, Qigong, tai chi, yoga, progressive muscle relaxation, jog-
ging, or even knitting.

What many of these techniques have in common
is that each takes your mind to a single focus point
whether it's to a repetitive chant or prayer, your breath-

ing, or integration of your breath with flowing muscle motion. Many of these practices have been around since ancient times with roots in many different cultures. These techniques have been passed down in the same way that delicious recipes get handed to the next generation. They have been practiced and honed, and in some significant way proven to enhance the quality of life for many millions of people. Unlike sports, there is no competition; no pressure to win or succeed. You are not trying to build endurance, break a sweat, or burn calories. The sole point is to enter a state of presence and mindfulness; not thinking about the past or the future.

Certain of these techniques do require training in order to prevent injury and learn proper technique— especially activities like tai chi, yoga, or Qigong. All are increasingly popular and effective ways to stay active, especially among seniors, but also provide significant relaxation benefits. Over time, there is no reason you cannot incorporate several methods into your life. But if you are a beginner to relaxation I recommend starting off with only one method. That way you can focus your attention on finding the relaxation within that specific meditative technique.

The following relaxation techniques do not require training or lessons to get started. Certainly, classes or workshops in meditation and visualization can help, but with the following simple steps you can start shifting the stress out of your life now.

Basic Meditation Technique from the Benson-Henry Institute

Before you start learning any of these techniques, I want to give a short word about practice. The phrase, "Practice makes perfect," is important, but please try not to think you have to be perfect. Do you have a hobby now that you are better at than when you started? Maybe playing an instrument, making jewelry, or playing a sport? How about in your job? Are you more skilled now than when you started? Of course you are. And you know why. Practice. It is going to be the same with every technique you learn to relieve stress. At first it may seem silly and not effective. But with practice I assure you that, just like Elaine, you are going to get better at it. With that in mind let's start with Benson's relaxation response technique.

Relaxation Response Technique

Pick a focus word, short phrase, or prayer that is firmly rooted in your belief system, and with which you are comfortable. Many people choose "one," "peace," "om,"

"Hail Mary full of grace," or "shalom," but use whatever works for you.

1. Sit quietly in a comfortable position.

2. Close your eyes.

3. Relax your muscles, progressing from your feet to your calves, thighs, abdomen, shoulders, head, and neck. This one takes some practice. Just think about releasing whatever tension you may feel in any of your muscles. Don't get stuck on this step or let it cause you more stress.

4. Breathe slowly and naturally, and as you do, say your focus word, sound, phrase, or prayer silently to yourself as you exhale.

5. Don't worry about how well you're doing at focusing on that word or phrase. At first it is natural for other thoughts to pop into your head, even things like: *This is stupid!* When other thoughts do come to mind, simply say to yourself, *Oh, well,* and gently return to your repetition.

6. Start with just a minute or two, but work up to more. When you can, continue for ten to twenty minutes.

7. When you are done just open your eyes and take in the world. The colors may seem more

vibrant. The sounds more noticeable. The world a little more peaceful. Just enjoy and appreciate the moments.

8. Do not stand immediately. (Remember, you probably have increased the amount of nitrous oxide gas in your body and lowered your blood pressure!) Continue sitting quietly for a minute or so, allowing other thoughts to return.

9. Practice the technique once or twice daily. Build in consistent but convenient times that work for you. Practice is important.

Guided Imagery

One way to attain a deep and relaxed state is to imagine yourself in a calming place like a beach or a mountain cabin. This is called *visualization*, or guided imagery. The idea is simple: Think about the sensory detail of the place you are in. Is it a warm, sunny day? Are brownies cooking in the oven? Are you wearing light, comfortable clothes? Perhaps you feel a warm breeze against your face or hear the breaking of tiny waves on the beach. As with meditation, you are able to observe the natural intrusive thoughts created by your brain's constant firing of neurons. But each time a random thought pops up, perhaps about the trip you need to make to the grocery store, or the thank-you card you need to write; instead gently hold your mind's focus either where you are in your visualization, or on your breathing. In the beginning this can be challenging, but with practice will become easier. You will also be surprised at how busy your mind is when you stop and observe it at work. Some people like to have a session with a trained professional or to use a CD. But you can just as easily put on some quiet music and guide your own visualization.

Journey to Relaxation

This is a technique, akin to visualization, that I use with my patients who may have a hard time imagining in a creative way, especially if they have never been to a relaxing place from which to draw memories. Adding the concept of a journey, which entails basic things like packing, helps them warm up the imagination, and relaxation occurs. I also suggest that it can be helpful for them to record the steps so they won't have to remember them.

1. Pick a quiet place to sit or lie down.
2. Position your body so that you are comfortable.
3. Take deep, even breaths for several minutes.
4. Then close your eyes, continuing a steady, mindful breath.
5. Do not struggle against your intrusive thoughts. They will naturally appear.

6. Simply observe them and let them pass.

7. *Stage 1 of your journey:* Start imagining packing your bag, knapsack, or suitcase with the few items you will need when you get to your destination: a comfy pillow, a blanket, comfortable clothes, and a pair of sunglasses. No need to take any shoes and if you want you can even imagine leaving them in the closet.

8. *Stage 2 of your journey:* Imagine taking your bag to the car, opening the door, and getting in. You don't even have to do the driving.

9. *Stage 3 of your journey:* Next, you are driving to your destination. As you breathe you can feel the muscles in your body begin to relax, as you get closer to a bridge.

10. *Stage 4 of your journey:* You are driving over the bridge toward your relaxing place, and as you cross and find yourself on the other side, you feel the car slowing down.

11. *Stage 5 of your journey:* You step out of the car and look around. You have arrived.

12. *Stage 6 of your journey:* Imagine yourself in a place that you associate with safety and comfort such as a familiar beach location, regular vacation spot, or forest cabin. Wherever you wind up notice that in that place there is the most relaxing and comfortable bed or couch

or chair you can imagine. This is your place of complete relaxation.

13. *Stage 7 of your journey:* Unpack your bag, take out the pillow, the blanket, feel yourself putting on the comfortable clothes and sunglasses and see yourself settling in that bed or couch or chair. You have found your place of complete relaxation.

14. When you are ready to leave simply reverse the stages, ending up by taking your shoes out of the closet and putting them on after you have put everything else away.

Practicing Mindfulness

Has this ever happened to you: You pulled out of the driveway, went in one direction, only to realize a few moments later that you didn't intend to go that way. You went that way because that's the way you usually go. Or perhaps you've been driving a familiar route and suddenly recognize you don't remember the last few minutes of your journey? Have you ever gotten off at the wrong floor from an elevator only to realize that's not the button you pressed? You just got off because the doors opened. These are instances where you were not mindful of the present moment. You were doing one thing, but thinking about something else.

Being mindful, or *present* means to keep your focus on what is going on at that very moment in your day. For instance, if you're brushing your teeth, you would keep your mind on that one task instead of making a grocery list in your head, regretting the years of black coffee you drank that yellowed your teeth, or obsessing about the deadline on the report due in tomorrow. You are brushing your teeth plain and simple, focusing all your thought energy on this task alone. This is practicing mindfulness. It sounds easy, but it's actually getting harder and harder to do. Just try it for a few minutes and see.

In today's world we pride ourselves on our abilities to *multitask,* doing two or more things at the same time. Some people are actually quite good at this. They can listen to the news, write e-mails, pack their kids' lunch boxes, and prepare for work all at the same time. But in this quest to become more productive and efficient, this sort of brain activity can actually create more stress. If you're serious about decreasing chronic stress in your life, the constant multitasking might have to be modified and mindfulness can help.

In fact, mindfulness is considered a well-respected meditation technique used to reduce stress. Experts call it Mindfulness-Based Stress Reduction (MBSR), and today there are many books devoted to teaching this simple but effective technique. Researchers are also able to study what happens inside a person's brain after they have learned MBSR techniques and put them to use. In a recent study, researchers at Massachusetts General Hospital recorded physical brain changes in subjects who underwent an eight-week mindfulness program. Using before and after MRI brain scans, the scientists could confirm increases in brain gray matter within the hippocampus, the area associated with memory, learning, and contemplation.

The hippocampus lives in your limbic system, that ancient part of our brain involved in fight, flight, or freeze. Among other things, it is responsible for memory, specifically consolidating short-term memories into long-term ones. This had an important survival component because it was important to be able to quickly distinguish between the signs of potential threat or potential benefit.

By using mindfulness we can enhance the connections between our limbic system and PFC. Mindfulness uses our PFC ability to modulate the deeper, more ancient structures of our brains. What you think really does affect what you feel, and even how you remember. Using your PFC *mindfully* helps you remember things more efficiently, which, as we all know, reduces stress. In Alzheimer's disease the hippocampus is one of the first parts of the brain to suffer damage, and the results are all too familiar: memory loss, difficulty laying down

new memories, and an inability to learn new information. Not remembering surroundings leads to disorien-
tation, a particularly stressful part of Alzheimer's that
leads to a lot of agitation among the unfortunate folks
suffering from this disease. You may have relatives with
this type of dementia and know how heartbreaking it
can be to watch them drift away from you day by day.
Once again, this type of research on mindfulness, and
other brain-based therapies, confirms our innate ability
to combat chronic stress naturally. And like any muscle,
our brain gets more powerful with practice.

The very word—*mindfulness*—makes you think of
a full mind, doesn't it? And there's nothing wrong with
a mind full of the ability to learn, remember, evaluate
oneself, and consider the perspective of others. This is
a fully functioning, healthy brain, rather than a brain
overwhelmed by worries, distractions, fears, and imaginary scenarios—the warning signs of chronic stress.
As you practice becoming mindful, or any of the other
exercises in this chapter, you will become keenly aware
of your ability to tap into your body's relaxation response whenever you need to.

How to Be Mindful: Stop, Look, and Listen

Mindfulness can be practiced for decades, or in a simple moment. Our brain is designed to compare information all the time, measuring one set of data against another. But in the process we sometimes overlook the simple wonder of being. Mindfulness is a way to relax by really living in the moment, not waiting for the next one.

A simple way to attain this involves being willing to slow down, to truly wake up and smell the coffee. The sequence is simple: Stop, look, and listen. When you *stop*, you give your brain a chance to appreciate what is happening here and now. When you *look*, you draw in the world around you into your inner world, and because you have stopped you can do this in a calm and thoughtful way. When you *listen*, you can hear the words of someone else, and because you have stopped and are looking, you can truly attend to how they feel, what they say, and how to help if you are being asked. This helps the other person feel valued, and feeling valued can decrease their own stress levels, cortisol, and increase their oxytocin. By using this simple technique, you can be more mindful, more effective, and thereby less stressed. And being around mindful people makes other people feel less stressed as well, so your mindfulness can have a great benefit to the other people in your life. Stop, look, and listen.

Mindful Moment Opportunities

With training, every moment becomes an opportunity to stop, look, and listen. But realistically if we can take even a few of these opportunities throughout the day to stop, notice, and take stock of what we are doing we can significantly reduce the stress of our everyday lives. Once you practice being present and mindful, you'll notice how much better you can focus, and how relaxed this makes you feel. Here are some common places where you can begin to integrate a few moments of mindfulness into your day.

In the car: We all drive a lot in this country, millions of miles a year. How many times have you driven somewhere, then wondered how you actually got there? We crank the music, plan the day, rehash it on the way back—often creating imaginary dialogues. We eat and drink, yell at our kids, apply makeup, chat and text on the phone. None of those miles are in a mindful state. Try stopping all that one day. No food, no sound, just a quiet, focused drive to your destination. Do not take your eyes off the road or your mind off the immediate task of driving. Go slowly and don't try to catch any lights. Let others pass you. Breathe, drive, and see how you feel. Be aware that every moment you drive you are approaching your destination.

At work: Whether working with the public or in the

back office with colleagues, we get easily caught up in work drama, most of which we have little control over but is a distraction. Mindfulness is about having an awareness and acceptance of what is going on and what is important. Stop, look, and listen. Be interested without being judgmental. As you become more mindful and aware, you can actually integrate more information, and produce more thoughtful solutions to a perceived problem. As you listen to your coworkers, listen for their point of view. They may not be practicing mindfulness, so they may still have a hard time doing what you are learning: to stop, look, and listen. As you become more attentive, you will feel less pressured to give a quick answer. In each situation, give yourself a few moments to reflect before you speak or respond to colleagues. As you slow down and listen, your coworkers may feel more understood, and may begin to do what you are modeling: to stop, look, and listen. Check in with yourself during the day to assess how you're feeling. You may be surprised how much calmer and in control you feel. And being in control is a great way to reduce the health risks that go along with stress. Mindfulness is being in control without a need to *take* control.

At home: Often we get home from work and feel we don't have the energy for a project, so we'll tune in to the computer or TV. It's quite habit-forming for many

Never Too Old to Learn

We often think, *With age comes wisdom*. But that's not always the case. Older people can also develop depression, anxiety, and stress. A recent British study, however, shows that people can experience the positive effects of mindfulness training at any age.

In the British team's research, twenty-two older adults were given an eight-week course in mindfulness-based cognitive therapy (MBCT). At the end of the training, they all reported improvements in emotional well-being including a decrease in stress and a more positive view of themselves. In fact, older adults scored higher on the observe-and-act-with-awareness tasks than their younger peers. Not only does this research support the already large body of evidence that mindfulness training works to reduce stress, it tell us that we're never too old to learn new tricks. Your dog maybe. But not you.

people. But instead of *plugging in* by checking your Facebook page, or watching TV, try *unplugging* by laying on the couch in silence or just reading a book. Try putting on some quiet music and doing nothing but listening. Sitting in a warm bubble bath will help you relax immeasurably. Do one quiet, unplugged thing and focus on that experience. Just as you stop, look, and listen at work or on the road, do the same for yourself. Check in with yourself, be aware of how your day went. Wonder about the moments of stress, why they happened, how you managed them, and what you will do differently next time. Being mindful allows your brain to use its PFC in a very practical and efficient way. And it just feels better to be less stressed out.

chapter 8

Creating a Stress-Reduction Plan

Harry had been a vice president at a large investment bank. He often worked a stress-packed eighty hours a week, traveled frequently, and slept little. The money was fantastic and he found himself on a constant thrill ride to close the next deal. But shortly after Harry turned thirty-eight, he was diagnosed with testicular cancer. While it was discovered in time for successful treatment, his doctor told him that if he continued with his current lifestyle, especially the high-stress job, the risk of recurrence might be higher. With a wife and two children to support, he agreed to a total lifestyle overhaul that would reduce stress in all areas of his life. Three years later, Harry works for the same firm, still with the same responsibilities, but with a different outlook on priorities. He has learned that his relationships are important in life. In fact, he has influenced the culture at work, and everyone there is happier and more productive. While it took a major life-changing event for him to be pushed into managing his time and getting in shape, the thrill that Harry gets from life now is that he and his family are very happy.

Self-Care to Reduce Stress

For far too many people it takes an illness to realize how our lives can become unbalanced by years of unchecked, chronic stress. We can't know if Harry's cancer arose because of his stress, but we do know that stress can lead our bodies into various states of ill health, both physical and mental. But why do we feel the need to push ourselves like this? How do we get caught up in a rat race of our own making? Why do we make poor health decisions when we know they're not good for us?

Certainly, we would never treat our children's health the way we treat our own. Would you give your kid a Snickers bar for lunch? Maybe, if you were stranded on a deserted island. But how often have you rationalized your own unhealthy behaviors by saying things like, "I just don't have time for the gym." We make sure our kids go to sleep on time, get exercise and fresh air. But at some point in our lives we stop doing this for ourselves. The result: chronic stress, ill health, and unhappy thinking.

In order to keep stress levels under your control, it's important to recognize that you need to stop and treat yourself the way you would treat your own children—you need to nurture yourself. This means taking care of yourself in a wise and careful way. Nurturing also means practicing some discipline, especially when that little voice inside whispers, *One more donut won't make a difference.* When you start on a course of self-nurturing, you are not spoiling yourself. Rather, you are practicing self-respect, self-control, and self-care, all of which help to balance your life and reduce stress over the long run.

Mood and Food

One of the most important aspects of self-care is what we eat and how we eat. Our bodies need to make tens of thousands of nutrients to survive, a combination of the basics like proteins and carbohydrates, with fats and oils, vitamins, minerals, and water. Throughout our evolution, we have adapted our bodies to the foods around us. But now, in our modern age of endless choice, the challenge to eat healthy has become formidable. Not only do we consume foods more varied and processed than at any other time in our history, we also have to fight our impulses to consume certain types of food when faced with stress.

Under a perceived stress the brain believes it needs to get more calories to prepare for the upcoming threat. Quick bursts of energy from mobilizing carbohydrates were preferable, especially if you had to run. Protein and other nutrients were hopefully already on board in the form of muscle and endurance, in case you needed to fight. Our bodies and brains have been trained like an Olympic athlete's to respond to the perception of life-threatening danger.

But as you know by now, today's perception of what is actually life threatening is usually wrong. The problem is, our stress response doesn't know that. When left unchecked and unrecognized, some of us develop dangerous habits connecting stress and food, basically conditioning ourselves the way Pavlov conditioned his dogs to salivate at the sound of a bell. This may be one of the reasons that the first thing to fly out the window when we're feeling stressed is our self-control when it comes to food.

This type of eating has nothing to do with hunger, and all to do with immediate gratification and escape. So you escape by treating yourself to something high in calories (carbohydrates) instead of foods from which it takes longer to extract nutritional value. This is such an ingrained phenomenon that a large part of food advertising is cleverly geared toward tempting you to consume just to make you "Feel better *now*!"

The reality, however, is that we usually regret consuming those potato chips, candy bars, and bacon double cheeseburgers, within moments of swallowing them. In fact, what can happen when we *escape eat* is that we are actually *increasing* our stress levels. First, when we eat foods for the sole purpose of making ourselves feel better, we are consuming unneeded calories. Those calories can put on extra pounds, which creates frustration and worry. Second, escape eating doesn't work. It doesn't generally solve the problems or assuage the feelings from which we sought the escape. So you wind up feeling worse; not only did you have that bad feeling to begin with, but you compounded that bad feeling by now adding guilt. Lastly, when we eat foods that physically tax our bodies, such as sugary sweets or high-fat snacks, we are contributing to internal stressors. Instead, you could be consuming the types of foods necessary for our bodies to handle the impact of stress.

What nutrition scientists believed for a long time, and now have solid research to support, is that different constituents in food can impact how you feel after you have eaten them. For instance, the components of nearly all foods influence blood sugar levels requiring the body to release insulin from the pancreas, which

The Jury Is Still Out on . . . Chocolate

Consumption of chocolate leads to a sugar high and swift increase in the release of serotonin, which makes people feel relaxed. This may be one reason that people think it alleviates depression. In fact, a recent study found that depressed individuals eat more chocolate than those who are not depressed. However, current evidence is mixed on whether chocolate really affects your mood or not. While the spike in serotonin caused by the carb content may temporarily improve mood, increased empty calories can also lead to weight gain. But if you want chocolate, better to grab some dark chocolate instead, with at least 70 percent cocoa. Research has shown you'll get healthy antioxidants when you eat dark chocolate. And that's something that can boost your mood for a long time.

helps move sugars to the cells that need energy. Certain foods also stimulate the release of brain chemicals that send messages throughout your body. These chemicals include mood-enhancing substances such as serotonin and dopamine, as well as natural stress-regulating hormones, such as norepinephrine and acetylcholine. It makes sense that certain foods have an impact on the brain. In fact, foods that are pleasurable to the brain can sometimes be addictive, like alcohol or maybe chocolate.

You've probably experienced the drowsiness of a post-Thanksgiving meal right? People often say that this is due to the chemical L-tryptophan found in turkey. In fact, turkey contains about the same amount of L-tryptophan as other poultry sources. The reason you feel relaxed, or drowsy after a big meal is that you most likely consumed a large load of carbohydrates along with the turkey. This combination—turkey (protein/ tryptophan) with the potatoes (carbohydrates)—enables the body to produce more serotonin than it would have with just turkey alone. It is the large dose of serotonin that has led you to a corner chair for a snooze.

Food chemistry is not only super interesting; you can apply it directly to your stress-reduction plan. Try learning about and choosing foods that work in tune with your body's natural stress-reduction ability, and avoid those that do not. Here are two lists—Have More and Have Less—to copy and practice until the knowledge becomes second nature. First, some food choices to include in your weekly diet and their stress-fighting constituents:

Have More

Complex Carbohydrates (whole-wheat breads and breakfast cereals, brown rice, vegetables): Carbs have a bad rap, but not all carbs are created equal.

While all carbohydrates signal the brain to produce serotonin, the feel-good chemical, only the
complex carbs supply you with a constant stream.
That's because they are digested more slowly,
unlike simple carbs that give you a spike of serotonin that promptly disappears. Also, when it
comes to stabilizing your energy, complex carbs
are your best options. When your energy levels
remain balanced, you are less likely to feel stress
than when they rise and fall throughout the day.

Also, some complex carbs fall into the "Super
Carb" category of antistress foods, like almonds.
Almonds have healthy levels of magnesium, a
mineral that helps regulate cortisol levels. A lack
of magnesium can make you more susceptible to
fatigue or headaches—just what you're trying to
avoid on your stress-reduction plan.

*Proteins (lean meats, poultry, fish, eggs, seeds and nuts,
tofu)*: While sugars are broken down into carbs
during digestion, proteins break down into amino
acids. Amino acids are the building blocks of
other enzymes, complex combinations of amino
acids that are the machinery of cells. Just as carbs
provide the energy to cells, amino acids supply
the energy for those machines. One of those amino
acids is called, *tyrosine,* and it stimulates the
production of natural stress-reducer hormones
dopamine and norepinephrine. Millions of years

ago, the release of these feel-good chemicals may have contributed to the amount of energy human beings were willing to spend on getting proteins. Hunting other animals was dangerous, but the protein reward must have been so great it outweighed the risk.

Omega-3 Fatty Acids (flax seeds, walnuts, salmon, sardines and mackerel, cooked soybeans): Studies have shown that omega-3 fatty acids decrease inflammation in the body. Two potent forms, DHA and EPA, have also been studied for their positive effect on a person's state of mind and show evidence that links consumption of omega-3s to better moods. Nutrition experts recommend a daily serving of omega-3s.

Vitamin C (citrus, strawberries, broccoli, bell pepper, strawberries, oranges, lemon juice, papaya, cauliflower, kale, mustard greens, and brussels sprouts): Current research suggests that vitamin C can reduce levels of stress hormones while strengthening the immune system. One study showed that cortisol and blood pressure levels returned to normal faster when people took 3,000 milligrams of vitamin C before a stressful task. If you have a particularly stressful event coming up, you may want to consider supplements, unless you're getting daily amounts of vitamin C by eating fresh, uncooked fruits and vegetables.

Eat Like the French

It's not just what you eat, but how you eat, that will contribute to reducing your stress. In France, people eat more slowly. The French make time for meals, and usually have several courses, one at a time. For instance, you might start with a soup, then have a small piece of fish or meat, then a small salad, and then a few servings of cheese and fruit. When you eat slowly, you are essentially stopping to taste and enjoy the food. This is a *mindful* act, during which you are nurturing yourself both physically and mentally. Slower eating and thorough chewing not only help with digestion, but numerous studies indicate that people feel full when they're supposed to. Fast eating, research shows, leads to overeating and becoming overweight. While most of us can't do a French-style meal every day, we *can* try to practice slower and more mindful eating, which goes a long way to easing stress. A final thought to go along with this tip: Eat with others. Making food and then sharing a meal also has amazing, stress-relieving effects.

Choline (egg yolks, soybeans, spinach, cauliflower, beef liver, salmon, wheat germ, peanuts, bananas): Choline is an essential nutrient and the newest member of the vitamin B group. Research has shown that low levels of B-vitamins, including B6, B9 and B12, may contribute to poor mood and feelings related to stress and depression. Choline helps synthesize acetylcholine, a brain chemical that is directly linked to memory and mental functioning. In fact, it is a deficiency of acetylcholine that is linked to Alzheimer's. Like vitamin C, B vitamins are water soluble so your body needs to consume them each day.

Fluids (water, herbal or noncaffeinated teas): In general, people need between 32 to 64 ounces of fluids each day. Proper hydration is needed for numerous body systems to work properly. One of the first symptoms of dehydration is a headache. Try to consume an adequate amount of fluids, avoiding beverages with high sugar content. Also, if you're on a stress-reduction plan, it's a good idea to avoid alcohol. It's a depressant, and can interfere with natural sleep patterns.

Have Less

Caffeine (coffee, tea, sodas, energy drinks): Caffeine is an addictive stimulant that wakes up your central nervous system. Many of us feel like we can't start our day without it. In moderate amounts, say about 250 milligrams (which equals about three 8-ounce cups of coffee), caffeine can usually be

harmless and even increase alertness. But overcon-
sumption leads to an overproduction of stomach
acid, causing digestive problems. Too much caffeine has also been linked to mood swings and
depression, and also can affect your ability to get
enough sleep. So go easy on the caffeine.

Simple Carbohydrates (white breads, refined cereals,
white rice, sweets, soda): Simple carbs break down
quickly into sugar. This results in a short burst
of energy as your blood sugar spikes. But that
spike goes down as fast as it went up leaving you
feeling tired, lethargic, and even irritated. If your
goal is to reduce stress, then sending your body
into a yo-yo of sugar highs and crashes will make
it much harder. Again, complex carbs work better
for long-lasting energy and balanced mood.

Sleep Right to Reduce Stress

Eating the right foods is just one part of nurturing yourself to reduce stress. Getting adequate and good quality
sleep is also vitally important. In fact, the more stress
you feel, the more likely it is that you are not getting
proper sleep. The lack of sleep then leads to impair-
ment of daytime functioning, according to sleep researchers at the Clayton Sleep Institute in St. Louis,

Missouri. In their recent study on the relationship between chronic stress and sleep problems, the investigators found that the greatest predictor of stress was in fact lack of sleep. So, while you may have a manageable amount of stress triggers in your daily life now, lack of proper sleep narrows your perspective and can make everything seem less manageable. Not only this, but lack of sleep additionally impairs your cognitive abilities and that can cause frustration, stressing you out even more.

Good quality sleep is so vitally important, yet people simply don't get enough of it. According to the National Sleep Foundation, about 70 percent of Americans are affected by a sleep problem, more than half of them with chronic problems. A big part of the problem is stress. When you lie awake at night worrying, you are not allowing your body the restful repose it requires. Too often we give sleep short shrift. We think that we can get by on fewer hours and so work harder or go to bed later. But sleep is not a luxury. While it may seem that nothing is going on as you lie there, the sleeping brain is actively reregulating all of the body's critical functions, from the immune system, to emotion and memory consolidation, muscle repair, and to growth, especially in children.

On average, people need approximately 8 hours of sleep to feel rested, although this varies from person to person and changes throughout your life. There are many people who feel rested after 6.5 hours of sleep, and they need not lie awake at night worrying that if they don't get 8 hours, they will be impaired. When it comes to sleep, experts suggest the amount of sleep a person needs can be assessed by allowing your body to wake naturally one day. Did you wake up after 7 hours and feel ready to start the day? If so, then 7 might be your number.

If you are having trouble going to sleep or sleeping, there are certain changes or behaviors—something the sleep experts call *sleep hygiene*—that are often recommended. While some may seem like common sense, you'd be surprised how often people ignore them. If you're serious about stress reduction, treat sleep like the sweet sanctuary it is.

Good Sleep Hygiene Tips

- Pick a bedtime schedule and stay with it. If you're tired earlier on some nights then go to bed, but try to choose a consistent bedtime.
- If noise is a problem, get a white noise machine, or fan so you don't have noise distractions.
- Avoid using alcohol as a sleep aid. It might help you become drowsy, but will interrupt your sleep.
- Don't drink caffeinated beverages after noontime. It takes about five hours for half the caffeine to

leave your system, so after ten hours you still have a quarter of that java or soda in your system, potentially interfering with your sleep. (For women on birth control it can take twice as long.) If you have to have an afternoon latte, then get decaf.

- Darken your room with shades or curtains so street lights and sun are adequately blocked.
- Try to avoid strenuous exercise or activities within a few hours before bedtime.
- If you're taking medications, ask your doctor or pharmacist if they can interfere with proper sleep.
- Finally, forgo rich and heavy meals within a couple of hours of going to sleep.

Organize Your Time

For some people, organizational skills seem to come naturally. Their homes are always neat. Their cars always clean. These folks are never late, and they never forget anything. I know two of them, but only two. Don't feel bad if you're a late bloomer in the organizational department. The good news is that there are many tools available to help you organize your time and your life. When we organize ourselves and manage

Feel Less Fright and Sleep Like a Baby Tonight

Do you think it's a good idea to let your kids watch sports like boxing or violent movies before bedtime? What about the horror-filled true-crime shows that fill prime time airwaves of network television today? Heck, the local news in some cities is even worse. Programs like these, as well as various frightening Internet links, immediately create a stress response at the same time we're trying to relax in order to get a restful bit of shut-eye. Your ancient brain is on alert: Who can sleep when danger is right in your living room, and creeping its way into your bed? You will probably not miss much more than the weather report if you skip the eleven o'clock news. What you will do is learn that you have control over whether to consume fear and stir up stress. In doing so you can maintain your calm, balanced nature. Once in bed, use that seven-stage journey to relaxation technique you learned in the previous chapter. Find that peaceful place and go to sleep. Don't forget your pillow and blanket.

our time well, we are reducing stress at various checkpoints through the day. There are always going to be curveballs that take you off schedule, but when you can assess what you're really capable of doing in a day, you won't try to squeeze in those extra things, which push your limits, and create episodes of needless stress.

Time management is often regarded from a business perspective as a way to become more productive. This is true to a degree. You can try to control how long it will take to accomplish a task. But in reality, we can't always know, we can't always control, and we have to be prepared for those "life happens" moments.

So I like to flip the idea of time management on its head. It's not about trying to control your time, but rather, how to prioritize according to what's really important. No stress-reduction plan can work until you take the time to consider how to spend your time. When we hit our daily targets of the most important tasks and goals, we will feel productive and incur less stress. Learn to let go of the feelings of frustration over small things that you ran out of time to do, like buying your sister a birthday card. Call her instead. She'd probably love to hear your voice.

It's also important to keep your everyday stuff organized. Your whole day can get thrown a wrench when you can't find your glasses or your keys in the morning. Make a *home* for your important odds and ends and put them back there at the end of the day. Again, we teach our kids these lessons all the time, but so often don't practice what we preach.

Here are a few habits to work on when time managing to reduce stress.

Time

Prioritize: What do you *really* need or want to accomplish today? Be brutal. Don't waste time and energy on tasks that are not really important at a particular moment. If you can't get to smaller tasks on a certain day, there is always *mañana* to repot the plants, or buy light bulbs. On another day, those will become a priority.

Make Lists: At the top of your daily list write the most important task of the day. Then list other items as they diminish in priority. This will help you from overbooking your day and help give you foresight about what you can realistically get done. Knowing in advance that you might not hit one or two of those things will go a long way toward reducing stress later on.

Say, "No": This is usually the hardest one for people to do because we not only want to accomplish a lot, but we want to please others. It's important to accept the fact that we simply cannot be in two places at the same time. We also cannot do two things at the same time very well.

Share the Load: Look at your daily list and see what you can delegate to someone else, or some *thing* else. For instance, you wanted to stop by the store to get flowers for a friend in the hospital, but there's no time. Use the Internet. Or, could your neighbor's teen take your dog for a walk so you don't have to rush home to do it? You can save yourself time, energy, and stress by simple delegations of tasks.

Stuff

Daily Tools: Where do you put your keys? Your bills? The remote control? Take a day to designate a place for those odds and ends that we can never seem to find and then become stressed over. A few hours organizing at home can save you weeks' worth of stress.

Eliminate Junk: Clutter and items you no longer need—like old magazines, empty jars, sweaters you've not worn for twenty years—take up both physical and mental space. In Chinese feng shui they say that you need to get rid of *old* in order to make room for *new*. I say get rid of the old to get rid of stress! A clutter-free desk or room will make you feel a lot more relaxed because you won't be burdened by the impending cleanup.

A final thought on time management and making priorities: The greatest asset we all have in our effort to reduce stress is: each other. Make sure that as you structure your time, and make your priorities, to be sure that you save time for people that matter to you. Notice here I don't say, "make," but *save*. This investment is a very

Emotional Housekeeping

Sometimes *emotional housekeeping* can follow actual housekeeping. I sometimes work with patients to organize and tidy up feelings and memories that are haunting or painful by creating an emotional attic. An attic is where you store pieces of your past like old photos, clothes, pictures, pieces of furniture, and presents from days gone by. A living room is where you live, where you come home and relax. But sometimes we have too much stuff in our living room, and we need to put it in the attic. Memories and emotions can be like that, cluttering up your living room and taking up your living space. For this you can create an emotional attic, finding a place for these pasts that have made you who you are.

good one, a way to reduce stress more than you can imagine.

Attitude and Positive Thinking

Do you ever wonder if optimistic people have less stress than those who are pessimists? You might think so, since the optimistic person usually looks less stressed perhaps than the pessimist. One of the latest developments in the field of psychology looks into such questions. This new movement, called *positive psychology,* studies the science of what goes right in human behavior, rather than what goes wrong. These psychologists seek to help people identify and actively create happiness by building upon people's natural strengths and by building their acumen in positive thinking. When it comes to relieving stress, there is some exciting new research coming out of the positive psychology movement that anyone can use, even a pessimist.

First of all, positive thinking doesn't mean naïve thinking, or that you have to *happy* your way through negative times. But on a day-to-day basis, the emphasis in positive psychology is that you learn to approach the adversity in a more positive and useful way. For instance, if you were given an assignment, something you'd never done before you might find yourself saying, "Wow, this is too hard," (and so "I can't do it" or "I feel stress because I can't do it . . . no, no, no"). Thinking positively, however, you might instead say, "This is a new challenge, and I'll give it my best shot." (Approach it like it's doable, and think *If I need help to accomplish it, I'll ask for help.*) Do you see the difference? I keep going back to the message we send our kids: Give it your best shot. We are all faced with daily challenges and obstacles. Our psychological success depends as much on our attitude as whether we can actually achieve a said task. In fact, your attitude influences your ability to accomplish and learn new things throughout your whole life.

Studies have shown that optimists, and people who engage in positive thinking, experience health benefits including lower rates of depression, reduced mortality from cardiovascular disease, even greater resistance to the common cold. Why this occurs is still a mystery. Some experts believe that when you have a more positive outlook on life, you are better able to cope with stress triggers. Over time, this would protect you from the harmful effects of chronic stress that you might otherwise accumulate. It's also believed that positive thinkers live a healthier lifestyle. They may follow a healthier diet, or may get more exercise. They are also less likely to drink or smoke in excess.

When you actively seek to create and embrace the happiness in your life, one of the beneficial side effects is going to be stress reduction. The key is how you find that happiness. The following are a few simple tips on how to do that from the positive psychologists.

Feel Gratitude

We all have something to be thankful for. Start your day with that thought and jot down or reflect on some of those things. These are usually the simplest things:

a hot shower, a car that starts, getting to the office on time, nice coworkers, a perfect cup of coffee, etc. When you stop to give thanks and experience gratitude you are actually changing your brain wave activity. You are focusing energy in a part of your psyche that produces feelings of value, of comfort, and acceptance, all of which are the antithesis of the stress reaction. We often say how important it is to "Count your blessings." This practical wisdom has never changed when it comes to relieving stress.

Find Meaning

Positive psychologists describe a meaningful life as one in which you are using your signature strengths and virtues in the service of something much larger than you are. One of the best ways to do this is to engage in activities that help others. Research backs up what most of us have learned to be common sense: Helping others makes us happy. In fact, a recent study by researchers from the London School of Economics found that the more the people volunteered, the happier they were. Whether you give time in church, community organizations, parks, or charity, it doesn't matter. You are using your strengths to provide service. When you make a contribution, you feel valuable. When you feel valuable, you have more confidence. Finally, when you

have more confidence, you feel happier and you cope
with stress better.

Focus on Your Strengths

If you received an award tomorrow and someone made
a speech about you, what are a few things they might
say? Perhaps you're someone with a good sense of hu-
mor, strong integrity, curiosity, kindness, or courage.
It's important to identify your strengths. Not only can
they help direct you to where to focus your efforts, they
also help you meet challenges. For instance, I'm a found-
ing member of our town's Educational Foundation. All
of our community members try to contribute in some
way. Because of my skills as a public presenter, I can
help represent the schools in certain ways that others
prefer not to. This is playing to my strength. On the
other hand, I would be creating stress and unhappiness
for myself (and probably my wife) if I tried to change the
oil in the car. Try choosing one of your strengths, and
think of a way to cultivate it this week. For instance, if
your strength is curiosity, then try to start up a conver-
sation with the new person at work or at the gym, or
invite a friend to the new exhibit at the museum. Your
strengths are a direct link to your inner confidence and
happiness, both of which are huge stress relievers.

Smile at a Stranger

When you smile, you are sending a message to others around you that you're relaxed and not a threat. People who smile present themselves as confident and content. These are people who are naturally attractive, because they suggest that whatever they are doing they are successful and happy. When you smile at others, you are indicating to others that you are not a threat to survival but an enhancement. Smiles are also contagious. What do you do when someone smiles at you? As humans we are designed to be social animals. When one member of the group smiles, we have a tendency to smile back without thinking. Whether or not someone smiles back is actually irrelevant. You'll feel much happier the more you smile anyhow.

A wise person once told me that there are really only two things you can control in your life: your attitude and your effort. Harnessing the power of positive psychology can help improve your attitude, increase your happiness level, create deeper meaning in life, and enjoy a greater connection with other people. When it comes to a solid, real stress-reduction plan, these are key elements that should go at the top of your list.

part VI

Severe Stress

chapter 9

Handling Severe Stress and Unexpected Stress Events

Frank was the father of four children and had a stressful job as the new mayor of a small city, which had been mismanaged for years. His attempts at making changes to get the city into the black were met with suspicion and personal attacks by entrenched city council members. It was a daily struggle for the young mayor whose wife was resentful because he was always stuck at the office. On top of his deteriorating marriage, Frank's teenage son dropped out of school and before long was arrested for petty theft. Frank's internist had prescribed him a mild sedative, which he thought might help the stress. But on the bad days, Frank started drinking scotch in the evenings to, in his words, "take the edge off." For months he thought he had it under control until one morning when his twelve-year-old found him passed out at the kitchen table. A week later, Frank walked into my office.

Frank didn't consider himself the type of person who would ever need a "shrink." His up-by-the-bootstraps, working-class background taught him to tough things out and if you sought treatment, especially for mental health issues, you were either weak or had some kind of serious mental illness. He didn't consider himself in either of those categories, yet here he was, with a troubled marriage, a son on the wrong life path, a difficult job, and a growing substance abuse problem. Naturally, Frank was anything but weak. He was courageous, willing to take on large responsibilities, and had high expectations of himself. He was also still a human being who found himself, like many other ordinary people do, under severe, unexpected stress.

There are infinite ways in which a person's stress levels can get out of control, pushing them into an emotional existence they no longer recognize. Further, choices like drinking, smoking, or other abuses, can begin to compound, pushing individuals deeper into despair and depression. Unfortunately, this is not an unusual development. In my practice I have worked with many individuals hit by the merciless curveballs of life: extended job loss, financial ruin and bankruptcy, family breakups, death of close relatives—especially a child—serious medical diagnosis, rape or other physical violence, lives turned upside down by natural disasters. This list goes on and on. And while the tipping points may be different from one person to the next, what is consistent is that unusual amounts of certain kinds of life stressors can be incapacitating.

When to Seek Professional Help

Most of this book has given you tips on how to manage stress yourself, first by recognizing and anticipating stressors, learning how to diffuse stress, relax, as well as by changing your perspective about the role of stress in your life. But in certain circumstances, these methods may not be enough. You do not need to be a hero, a soldier, or an army of one. If stress seems overwhelming follow this rule: Never worry alone. It may be lifesaving to get professional help and even life threatening if you or a loved one does not.

In Frank's story above, he had become aware of an increased level of stress and sought help from his physician. He bristled at the idea of meditation or exercise. Meditation seemed too weird, he thought, and he didn't need to lose weight. The idea of a quick fix in the form of a mild sedative seemed much simpler. The quick fix was for *just* a little extra stress. It never occurred to him to make some life changes such as limiting after-office meetings and conferences, making weekend time for his family, doing homework with his kids, or having a regular date night with his wife. Frank was a modern twenty-first century citizen—he just took on more responsibilities. He earnestly told me he had no time to take care of himself. The thought of not getting his work done was too stressful. He was skipping meals, not getting adequate sleep, getting no exercise, and now he was making the choice to take a narcotic as well as increasing amounts of alcohol to handle his stress. The result: His passing out on the kitchen table.

Ashamed, he sat across from me in our first session, and said he should be stronger, smarter, and more productive. Instead he felt like a lousy dad and a distant husband. His wife had assured him he was neither, and his children—even the teenager—simply wanted their father back. With the support of his family, and a willingness to share his worry, he had found his way to my office. In fact, research indicates that the support of family, or of other people in your life, has an enormous impact on relieving stress. A 2011 study from the University of Maryland recently showed convincingly that men whose families were supportive were more likely to initiate and continue in substance abuse treatment.

The proverbial last straw of using drugs and alcohol to escape his stress—his overwhelming stress— may have seemed a solution. But, as is often the case, the solution had started to become the problem. Frank found himself wondering how he got from "there" to "here," and acknowledged he could not get back to "there" without professional help.

You might relate to this set of challenges differently. Stress can reveal itself in many ways, depending on your personality, age, background, or gender. Some people are quick to experience the fight response, and become aggressive and irritable. Some become incapacitated by flight, and instead feel fearful and anxious. And some become frozen, mired in a withdrawn world of indecision and depression.

Whatever the result of compounded stress, too often people worry alone, perhaps ashamed of appearing too weak to deal with their problems. They feel they should be able to cope by indulging in various types of behaviors. But what they are really doing is avoiding their issues altogether. Like Frank, their choices ultimately create more stress. In a bitter irony, another problem is created, along with another failed solution.

Stress and Substance Abuse

As Frank discovered, when people feel overwhelmed it often seems easier to avoid dealing with severe stress by using substances such as alcohol and various medications, legal and otherwise. This avoidance is an unfortunate and frequent strategy. But every time you use drugs or alcohol to avoid a problem you are simply convincing your brain that you are not strong enough, smart enough, or capable enough of even coping with the problem, let alone solving it. As you become less sure of yourself, and more reliant on avoidance, your anxiety goes up, your stress increases, and you use drugs and alcohol to avoid those feelings as well. The slippery slope has begun.

In fact, substance abuse is often an avoidance, rationalized at the beginning, as a *coping method*. There is so little confidence in oneself to confront and deal with highly stressful emotional events of the past. This is not about courage, but about self-doubt and a lack of self-worth and value. It is not uncommon, particularly in people with psychiatric conditions, to feel overwhelmed by their challenge and unable to cope. Research has shown that at least 50 percent of people with substance abuse problems also have a coexisting psychiatric condition such as depression, PTSD, and other challenges.

But even in the absence of an underlying psychiatric challenge or catastrophic event, individuals can still find themselves slipping into unhealthy substance abuse habits. As one of my patients, a recovering alcoholic recalled when he first turned to alcohol, "I'd just have a couple shots to take the edge off." This does not mean that everyone who turns to alcohol or other substances becomes alcohol or drug dependent. There is no *standard* course to arriving at a drinking problem. But every alcoholic or addict starts somewhere. Whether or not you or your loved ones could become addicted depends on many factors including life circumstances and genetics.

What distinguishes an alcoholic from a person who abuses alcohol is that the dependent person has a physical need to drink every day. They experience withdrawal symptoms without the substance. In fact, alcohol withdrawal can be a life-threatening emergency, resulting in seizures and even death. These individuals suffer from addiction and will frequently try to hide it from others, sometimes "successfully" for years.

People who abuse alcohol don't have the same physical need to drink, but they do drink excessively on a regular basis and their drinking interferes with their lives. They may use alcohol or other substances to avoid or escape managing unpleasant emotions, and their behavior to others may appear as that of an alcoholic, even if they are not actually dependent. Despite the degree, substance abuse is just that—abuse of a substance. It's not good for you, your family, or any of your relationships, and it does not help people manage severe stress and problems in life. Rather, substance use disorders can exacerbate problems. If any of the following occurs, you should seek professional help immediately:

- Repeated failure to fulfill work, school, or home responsibilities.
- Abuse of substances in high-risk situations such as in a vehicle or operating machinery.

- Abuse-related legal situations, such as a DUI arrest, disorderly conduct, or damaging property.
- Continued substance abuse despite ongoing relationship problems either caused or worsened by drinking or substance abuse.

Today, perhaps the most widely studied and accepted screening for alcohol abuse is called the CAGE Questionnaire. First published back in 1984, it asks four simple questions:

1. Have you ever felt you should cut down on your drinking? Yes or No
2. Have people annoyed you by criticizing your drinking? Yes or No
3. Have you ever felt bad or guilty about your drinking? Yes or No
4. Have you ever had a drink first thing in the morning to steady your nerves or get rid of a hangover (eye-opener)? Yes or No

Ratings:
0–1: No apparent problem
2 or more: Clinically significant

This simple study is remarkably accurate. Be honest with yourself, and get some help if you score 2 or more.

What Doctors Don't See

Many people assume that the family doctor would be able to detect substance abuse among patients, especially regular patients. Yet fewer than one in three primary care physicians thoroughly screen their patients for substance abuse problems, including alcohol, according to a national survey by the National Center on Addiction and Substance Abuse at Columbia University. The same survey showed that about four in ten patients said they had a substance abuse problem that went undiagnosed, while one in ten said his or her physician knew they had a substance abuse problem but did nothing to address it.

This is not necessarily news to doctors. In the same survey, fewer than 30 percent of the doctors considered themselves very prepared to identify alcoholism or drug use. Many physicians are not trained to spot clues for substance abuse, and substance abusers can be very discreet. As a result, many people become at risk of not getting the help they may need. So if you have a loved one whom you suspect is getting in trouble with substances, consider going with them to the next doctor visit, or encourage them to seek help from someone trained in addiction medicine.

Eating Disorders

Drugs and alcohol are not the only substances that people turn to in their attempt to escape severe stress. For some individuals, food is the substance that either can't be controlled or is used as a proxy for control. In general, eating disorders are marked by extremes such as dangerous reduction of food intake as is the case with anorexia nervosa or purging back the eaten food with bulimia. Or, the opposite, extreme overeating, is also perceived as a coping method. Binge-eating disorders, which are more common than anorexia, can affect 2.8 percent of the population according to recent National Institutes of Health statistics, with the average age of onset at twenty-five years old.

Researchers have found stress can have a powerful effect on your appetite and food cravings. Yet the specifics of how cortisol levels trigger one person to overeat and another to stop eating is still being investigated. Stress seriously affects the way your body chooses healthy foods, how you digest those foods, and how you absorb nutrients. An unhealthy diet or lack of nutrition contributes to stress. This stress in turn contributes to a continued poor diet, and the vicious cycle perpetuates.

What is well documented, however, is that people with extreme food disorders also suffer from coexisting psychological conditions including anxiety, depression, and personality disorders. According to a recent nationwide survey published in the *Journal of Biological Psychiatry,* more than 94 percent of people with bulimia, 56 percent of those with anorexia and 79 percent of those with binge-eating disorder had at least one other psychiatric diagnosis.

Any type of extreme eating behaviors such as anorexia, bulimia, or binge eating is a clear call for professional intervention. Untreated eating disorders can lead to a host of health problems that include malnutrition, muscle atrophy, chronic fatigue, diabetes, seizures, organ failure, and heart disease to name just a few. In fact, eating disorders have the highest mortality rate of any psychiatric condition. Because these conditions, as with most other types of substance abuse, are associated with other psychological disorders, specialized, long-ranging treatment is recommended.

Suicidal Thoughts

Severe stress can truly be lethal. Though we evolved the stress response to survive, stress itself can drive us to want to end our lives. High levels of stress can leave us feeling so powerless that there seems no way to immediately cope; no action except that of extreme avoidance of the stressor, of reality, of life. In most people, this feeling is fleeting, and many of us may have envisioned ourselves in the throes of wanting to end it all.

But fleeting means just that, and the next second or so you are back in life, perhaps still stressed, but not seriously thinking of ending your existence.

But if those thoughts persist, I encourage you to seek professional help immediately. Persistent thoughts of ending your life is an emergency and not to be ignored. Whether you seek a counselor, clergy, psychiatrist, or psychologist, it is paramount that the person is professional. This is not a job for friends and family, although their ongoing understanding and support will be imperative. Family or friends should help you get to a professional, not try to *be* the professional. To get the help you need, please go to someone who manages this degree of stress as part of his or her job. Suicide is not an option to deal with stress, no matter the magnitude.

As a psychiatrist, I am biased. From my point of view it is never too soon to seek professional help. But finding the time to get to a counselor may be impractical, and may cause you even more stress. Yet, just like meditating, exercising, and any other way in which you take care of yourself, having a professional in your therapeutic corner can be lifesaving when needed, and can help provide a deeper understanding of who you are and why you do what you do. While being suicidal is the most extreme example of a need for psychiatric care, why wait for it to get that desperate? Take a proactive approach in handling stress.

Who to Consult for Help

Licensed Mental Health Professionals When dealing with the impact of severe stress in your life or that of a loved one, choosing a caregiver can be challenging, which is why it is a good idea to do your research so you can be sure they can provide the proper help. There are a wide variety of specialists who come from different academic disciplines but share knowledge of the causes of psychological distress and its treatment. Each profession has its own strengths, with varying depths of training, knowledge, and expertise. You will want to be sure that anyone you seek for treatment has been properly licensed to practice.

> **Psychiatrists (MD, OD)** are medical doctors who have graduated medical school and specialized in psychiatric disorders. Psychiatrists are state licensed and generally covered by health insurance. Psychiatrists treat patients in hospital settings, community settings, and may be in a practice with other professionals. Their medical training and licensure grant them the privilege of prescribing medications, and in many cases also provide different psychotherapies, such as insight oriented, cognitive behavioral, motivational, and others. Psychiatrists generally hold

the final responsibility for a patient in a multi-disciplinary team. A board certified psychiatrist means they have passed examinations offered by monitoring associations designed to identify qualified specialists.

Psychologists (PhD, PsyD, EdD) have earned a doctorate degree in psychology. Many hold state licenses to treat patients and are covered by health insurance plans. Only psychologists in Louisiana and New Mexico can prescribe medications, but in every state they provide psychotherapy and may also do psychological testing as well as research.

Psychiatric Clinical Nurse Specialists (CNS) are registered nurses (RN) who then earn a master's in advanced practice specializing in psychiatric services. They often provide psychotherapy, are usually covered by health insurance, and may prescribe some medications under the supervision of a psychiatrist (MD).

Clinical Social Workers (LICSW) will generally hold a master's degree in social work. Many are licensed to treat patients and are covered by health insurance plans. They provide psychotherapy and are trained particularly to focus on a person's interactions with the family or wider community. They do not prescribe medication.

States also license a variety of other master's-level counselors with various areas of specialization.

Psychodynamic Therapies

Insight-Oriented Psychotherapy

When people go to a professional to talk, or go into therapy, most often this refers to *talk* therapy, and any of the practitioners above may do this type of intervention. This is not at all like talking to a good friend or family member. Highly trained, and able to help a person develop insight into why they do what the do, this form of therapy has its roots in Freudian psychoanalysis. It is one of my personal favorite forms of therapy to do with a patient, as it allows for an incredible self-awareness, and often an enormous relief from stress. The young mother who overcame her "paralyzed" arm was doing insight-oriented psycotherapy.

Cognitive Behavioral Therapy

This form of therapy is based on the idea that what you think affects what you feel, and that what you perceive affects what you think. For certain conditions, this can be a terrific therapy for symptom reduction. Cognitive behavioral therapy (CBT) attempts to correct deep-seated patterns of negative thoughts and behaviors, and as the name implies, has two parts. The cognitive therapy part helps people break patterns of thinking that contribute to fears or depression, and other unsuitable responses. The behavioral therapy part helps people change their response to those thoughts.

For instance, a person with severe anxiety might be afraid to drive because they think they will get in an accident. This is *negative thinking* that can keep a person from driving or even riding in a car, due to the anxiety they then *feel*. As a result, this person might then avoid invitations to attend social events, or get-togethers with friends or family. These are examples of *negative behavior,* the result of a thought that has led to a feeling of anxiety. The goal of cognitive behavioral therapy is to break this negative circle of thoughts and behaviors that can become so emotionally crippling. CBT can also be very effective in our day-to-day routine, even if we are not at our stressed-out max. Just recognizing that what you think has an effect on what you feel shifts the brain into PFC mode in which you can make decisions that lead to reducing stress.

It's not unusual for negative thoughts to surface when people are under stress. As you've learned, stressors cause our bodies to react with the fight-or-flight-or-freeze response. With CBT, the first step is to help you recognize when you're stressed. Because recognition is a cognitive, thinking process, it moves us out of the limbic, feeling part of our brain back to the PFC where we analyze information and make decisions based on that analysis. Having an *inner regulator,* or personal stress scale, can signal just how stressed you really are and help you turn down the volume. This is especially crucial for people who are under severe stress, and who have perhaps lost the ability to balance rational with irrational reactions to stress.

Typically, there are three components to a stress reaction. First, in order for stress to be activated, a person has to perceive some threat or danger in the environment. Secondly, that trigger has to be evaluated and interpreted to mean something is going to happen as a result of a belief. This belief can be rational or irrational. The activation and belief then lead to a consequence in the person, an emotion or behavior in response to the perception. In cognitive behavioral therapy these are commonly called the ABCs: Activation, Belief, and Consequence. Ultimately, we all respond to the environment with the same basic mechanisms, but not all of our responses are based on a rational belief. For example, some people are terrified of elevators, unable to overcome the fear that, when trapped in such a small space, bad things will happen From an evolutionary point of view this may make sense: if you are in a dangerous situation you need space and an ability to run away, not easy things to do in the confined area of an elevator. But rationally, it is highly

Grief and Mourning

Grief and loss is a fact of life that everyone faces at one time or other. Grief and mourning are well studied, starting with the groundbreaking work done by Elisabeth Kübler-Ross in her 1969 book *On Death and Dying*. The five stages of grief that she described are now known to come in many forms, in any order, and can often repeat.

- Denial (and isolation)
- Anger
- Bargaining
- Depression
- Acceptance

Sometimes the intensity of feeling, however, seems intolerable, and emotions can become uncontrollable. Most clinicians agree that a year of grief and mourning is expected and acceptable. A person in mourning typically goes through the five stages, usually more than once, and in any order.

But if this goes on for more than a year, people like me start to worry, as grief in this case becomes what is referred to as *pathological*, or *complicated*. People in mourning who get to a counselor before this sets in have much improved chances for successful treatment. When grief does becomes entrenched, various treatments can and should be used, including counseling, cognitive behavioral therapy, other psychotherapies, and possibly the temporary use of medication. In extreme cases where safety has to be maintained, an inpatient psychiatric hospitalization may be needed.

unlikely that anything bad will happen while you are traveling up or down from one floor to another. CBT explores the connection between thought, feeling, and behavior, with the belief that if you can change the thought you can change the feeling and therefore the ensuing behavior. Even more, perception itself leads to thought, which leads to feeling. If you can change the perception that an elevator is a dark dungeon of doom, you can change the thought and feelings that follow.

According to a recent meta-analysis published in the *Clinical Psychology Review,* CBT was shown to be effective for many types of disorders resulting from stress. These included large effects for depression, anxiety, panic, social phobias, and PTSD. CBT even had moderate effects on marital conflict, anger, some of the imaginary aches and pains of children, and chronic pain. CBT is truly a brain-based therapy. We have powerful brains, ones that can intensify anxiety and depression, which may result in response to perceived stress. But the same brain that escalates those feelings can also retrain itself to reduce them.

Medications In certain cases of severe stress—such as complicated grief, PTSD, or depression—medication may be recommended. Fortunately, our profession can provide a greater variety of more specifically targeted medications for severe stress disorders than ever before. Having said that, not all medications work for each individual and frequently there is some trial and error involved, not to mention certain side effects. Also, medication alone is typically less effective than a combination of psychotherapy and medication. All medications require a prescription.

The types of medications that one would receive will depend largely upon a person's diagnosis. In general, most psychiatric medications target brain cells or neurons. These neurons communicate via chemicals called neurotransmitters (NTs) that send messages from one cell to another. Psychiatric medications can be broadly simplified to either boost NTs when there is a lack, or to block an abundance of NTs when there are too many.

In the case of depression, for instance, NTs like serotonin and norepinephrine are involved, and often they are lacking. As such, depression is commonly treated with medications called SSRIs, or serotonin reuptake inhibitors, which today have household names such as Prozac, Zoloft, and Celexa. Certain types of depression may alternatively be treated with SNRIs, or serotonin/norepinephrine reuptake inhibitors. These are better known by their brand names such as Effexor, Remeron, and Cymbalta.

For patients experiencing various types of anxiety, your doctor may prescribe any one of the group of benzodiazepine medications such as Xanax, Valium, Klonopin, or Ativan. These are minor tranquilizers and work on the central nervous system and a neurotransmitter called GMBA to help you decrease anxiety and feel relaxed. Unlike antidepressants, which can take weeks to work, these medications, work quickly, having a direct effect on the electrical conduction of the brain cells. Within an hour or less, you can feel the anxiety melting away.

When taken as directed, benzodiazepines can be incredibly helpful and effective because these medicines work so fast and give such relief. But they are also very addictive. When taken outside of medical supervision without a prescription, or obtained through a friend or a drug dealer, they can be very dangerous, as benzodiazepines are very powerful neurochemicals. If you are prescribed one, please be sure to take it as your physician instructs.

Sometimes medication is a critical part of therapy. Administered wisely and judiciously, and taken as directed by your physician or nurse practitioner, it can have remarkable and even lifesaving effects. The experience of severe stress is vivid and sometimes may feel too overwhelming to wait for the talking and cognitive behavioral therapies to work. But if you are going to take any medication, I urge you to go to a psychiatrist first. People like me have devoted our careers to helping those with profound stress. It is an incredible honor and privilege to help someone in their time of need. As you will see in the next chapter, in situations of less severe stress, the type we may encounter just going to work, driving home, or paying the bills, how we respond to each other's stress can have a huge impact as well.

part VII

Reducing the Stress of People Around You

chapter 10

How to Become
a Stress Expert

When Zelda won a community volunteer-of-the-year award she was thrilled. All of her hard work and dedication had been appreciated. But her joy quickly turned to fear when she heard that the award would be presented in front of an audience and that she would be expected to say a few words. To Zelda, a friendly but shy person, nothing was more terrifying than speaking in front of a group. So she told the organizers she couldn't do it. But instead of letting her opt out, they decided to help her through it. They would provide a podium she could stand behind, and position some of her associates right next to her so she wouldn't be alone at the front. They also offered to help write her speech and to practice with the microphone. When the day came, Zelda was still afraid but not terrified. When she got up to make her thank-you speech and looked at the faces of her helpers nodding and smiling, she felt confident. Zelda received the award, but finding the strength to deliver her speech became one of the most unforgettable moments of her life.

Whether the moments are small or large in another person's life, you can have a profound effect on other people's experiences, especially their stress levels. Zelda was lucky. The organizers understood that public speaking is hard for some people. Not only did they empathize with Zelda's fear, they thought of ways to minimize her stress. Whether you're aware of your ability to help alleviate another person's stress or not, it is likely you have done it without knowing you're doing anything more than being thoughtful, kind, or neighborly. It's important to recognize that those things really do matter when it comes to relieving individual as well as societal stress.

In fact, our brain chemistry is actually altered when we help others, or they help us. You feel good when another driver allows you to proceed first. Someone else feels good when you hold the door open for him or her. You feel better when you make a donation of time or money to a cause that's important to you. If cortisol is the *Minutemen* of stress hormones then oxytocin is what I'll call the "Nobel Peace Prize." And it is oxytocin, also a hormone, which is released by the brain when people receive help from another human being, as well as offer help. Even the *perception* of emotional support induced the release of oxytocin according to a comprehensive review by researchers from Cedars-Sinai Medical Center in Los Angeles of 102 oxytocin studies conducted between 1959 and 2009.

This remarkable hormone was found to create a general sense of well-being including calm, improved social interactions, increased trust, and reduced fear, all of which are critical stress-reducing factors. Beyond helping us to feel respected, valued, and loved, oxytocin has also been shown to have significant effects on our health. Blood pressure is reduced, the desire to be with other people is increased, and social exchanges are enhanced. So, your direct actions, small and large, can increase oxytocin in others, which in turn reduces their stress, and improves their well-being. That was undoubtedly the experience of the organizers who helped Zelda through her stressful public speech. You *also* benefit chemically when you adopt and practice this kind of pro-social, PFC awareness in various parts of your own life.

Home Sweet Home

When you hear the words, "There's no place like home," you automatically think of Dorothy from *The Wizard of Oz* clicking the heels of her ruby_red slippers. The words conjure a warm and comforting sentiment that we assume most people share. But when it comes to reducing stress, it is particularly important that the place you and your family members go to for sanctuary at the end of the day is indeed restful and comfortable. In chapter 8 we discussed the importance of keeping stuff organized, as a way to decrease your daily stress triggers. Yet, on a scientific level, how you keep your nest in general can impact the levels of cortisol in your in body.

In a recent UCLA study, researchers conducted a series of home tours of dual-income couples. With both partners working, this particular group assumes a certain income level, as well as limits on time they could spend keeping the home up. Using sophisticated language-analysis software, the wives' descriptive words were correlated with their cortisol levels. The researchers then calculated the frequency of words such as "clutter," and "unfinished," as well as restful words, and nature words to measure their home stress. They discovered that the women who described their homes as restorative were happier and healthier. But women with scores that suggested higher home stress had measurably greater levels of cortisol. Higher cortisol levels means higher health risks.

We have no way of knowing if happier people keep a neater or more comfy home, but what this research tells us is that we do have some control over the levels of stress of other people in the home. If you think about it for a minute this is really common sense. Have you ever been to someone's home where there is a long unfinished DIY project that obstructs everyone's lives, like a half-finished bathroom, stairway, or porch? Who wants to take a daily detour and obstacle course just to take a shower? What about in homes where you cannot find anything without a GPS tracking device? Now that's stressful.

Life is full of enough work-arounds that you can't control, so you don't want to chock your homelife full of them. The kids fight over the bathroom and TV, clothes pile up on the laundry room floor, and unsorted mail is strewn all over the kitchen counter. Sound familiar? It is no wonder that it is the wife whose cortisol is high, as the burden of controlling and organizing often and unfairly falls on her shoulders. And when she's working full time, these tasks present themselves as additional work. Yet, each home has solutions in the way of a schedule, responsibility, and contribution list.

My advice: Create a family routine and share the responsibility as much as you possibly can. Some of the most relaxed and successful people I know have something like a *First Saturday*. Each month, part of the day is dedicated to home organization. This small commitment of several hours a month can go a long way toward

Why Superheroes Always Get the Girl

Men and women are often attracted to various exterior attributes in the opposite sex such as bulging muscles or bosoms. But when it comes to selecting a mate, surprising inner qualities also find themselves high on the list. New research from the University of Nottingham in London suggests that traits of selflessness and altruism may have evolved genetically over time because such qualities were desirable when it came to reproduction.

In the study, seventy identical and eighty-seven non-identical female twin pairs completed questionnaires relating to their own levels of altruism (e.g., "I have given money to charity."), and how desirable they found this in potential mates (e.g., "Once dived into a river to save someone from drowning."). Results revealed that genes influenced differences in both the participants' preference toward a mate and their own altruistic behavior. "The expansion of the human brain would have greatly increased the cost of raising children so it would have been important for our ancestors to choose mates both willing and able to be good, long-term parents," said lead researcher, Dr. Tim Phillips.

From this evolutionary perspective it would also follow that people with superhero traits would be highly desirable and thus have many offspring for whom they hold themselves responsible. Now technically, taking care of your own kids is not altruism as it directly influences your long-term success. But the trait of giving to others is indeed a good indicator of the type of person you are, and how you assign your priorities. And so it would make evolutionary sense for a female to seek such qualities in a mate, as survival was hard enough without having to also care for offspring. When a behavior is selected for based on mating, it has been given a special name by scientists who are interested in this sort of thing: *sexual selection*.

Sexual selection has a powerful effect on the transmission of genes from one generation to the other. Traditionally, superheroes are particularly altruistic, and are often perceived as extremely desirable mates. In the comics, they're too busy saving the world. But in reality, most superheroes may actually be more like Clark Kent, faithfully coming home at night, or giving their kids a hug and "I love you" before they go off to school. *Bottom line:* Giving of oneself to others has been favored by sexual selection. The ability to reduce each other's stress is in our genes.

reducing family stress. When the nest is neat, everyone's cortisol levels are reduced. A relaxed parent can lead to a relaxed kid. There are days when the home feels chaotic of course. But it makes sense to all work together for the same goal—to make your home a home sweet home.

You can also do this without feeling you have to overhaul your house. It is just a small change of perspective. As a family, you are not just fixing up the house because it's a mess. Rather, you are making an investment in creating a restorative place that nurtures your emotional and physical health, decreasing your stress and the stress of everyone else in the home.

Work Stress-Free

Unlike your home, you have very little control in the workplace, even if you are in senior management. We don't all get the big, sunny corner office, the superergonomic chair, or four weeks of vacation. Perhaps most important, we don't usually get to pick our work associates. Indeed, it often comes down to what your coworkers do, or fail to do, that can cause the most stress. If any of you are TV watchers, you may have seen the hit comedy series, *The Office*. Steve Carrell plays the overconfident but inept supervisor who messes up everyone's plans. When we see these hilarious depictions of office bickering, bungling, and sabotage, we laugh, because we've somehow all had a boss with inane qualities, and we've all been witness to inappropriate office behaviors.

But in real life, much of what we lump into the category of *office politics* isn't funny at all, and is in fact very stressful. Office politics rates at the top of the list in many management polls as the aspect of work that induces the most stress. On average, people just want to do a good job and be valued for their work. They prefer not to get caught up in office intrigues, or be forced to work with difficult people, and they resent when supervisors play favorites when no merit is involved. In work settings where office politics run amok, the risk for an uncivil environment rises while productivity falls. In one recent study of nurses in Texas, scientists compared working environments that were viewed as civil and uncivil. The nurses who worked in settings with higher workplace incivility took significantly more sick days. To be exact, this amounted to approximately $11,581 per nurse per year. But the personal cost of working in a hostile and unsupportive place is incalculable for those who find themselves there. Who wants to work in a place like that? Thankfully, you have some influence on what is going on around you.

While one person may not be able to change an entire office culture, what you can do is focus on the group you work with most closely day to day. Within this circle, you can influence stress levels before they ricochet around to you. Try the following.

Exercise: Thank and Connect

Pick a coworker who seems to have a hard time handling stress. You know who they are. Put their name on a piece of paper. Underneath the name I want you to create two categories. The first is "Thank," the second is "Connect."

Now, in the "Thank" column you will write:

1. How does this person help me do my job?
2. How does this person help the company perform better?
3. Acknowledge three (3) things this person does that I, or our group appreciate(s).

Under the "Connect" column write the following from your knowledge:

1. Their full name.
2. Details of their lives you know.
3. Three (3) questions you could ask to know them better.

Once you jot down the lists, you are going to assign yourself the small tasks laid out in number 3 of each column. First, when the opportunity presents itself, you are going to go out of your way to make sure that the person is thanked for their efforts. You probably already thank them reflexively for ordinary things such as bringing back a stapler they borrowed. But when they do that, give them an extra thanks for being the last one to stay the other day, or cleaning off the table in the conference room, or starting a meeting for you when you were running late. Whatever it is, when you offer that extra thanks, you are conveying that you noticed their effort (even if it is part of their job), and that you *value* them.

The same thing goes for the Connect list. You may ask a question that allows you to know them better. This could be about where they went on vacation, how many kids do they have, have they ever been to Disney World? Those are not deep, personal questions, but they do reveal information about their lives and open the door for follow-up questions and better knowledge. By asking, you are connecting. You are conveying to them that you are interested in them as a human being, and that you value them. Now, do the same for another person, and then another.

So what, you may be wondering, does Thank and Connect have to do with minimizing stress? It's simple. When we make the effort to show others they are valued, you are practicing respect. Of all the human desires and needs, I think that feeling respected is one of the most fundamental. You can relieve someone's stress simply by showing them they are valued and respected for their work and who they are. Stress and anxiety make people feel insecure and unsettled, and in the extreme, very angry. But when people feel valued and respected by others, they relax and let down their guard. Their cortisol levels decrease, and they move in the opposite direction of stress. While you can't remove every stress trigger from your colleagues' lives, you can still influence their stress levels by practicing Thank and Connect. Try it and see what happens.

School and Youth Stress

Whether or not you are a parent, it's important to recognize that the foundation of many of our earliest stress triggers, and the way we learn to handle them, develop in our youth, and often revolve around school. This is the time that we are learning to navigate the complex social grid, decipher personalities, and become popular, while at the same time deal with family issues and the common developmental norms of parental separation. And let's not forget the academic pressures. Many of us recall those years—the *acne era*—as somewhat fraught, and might loathe having to revisit them. But we made it through even though it seemed remarkably horrible at the time.

I bring this up in all seriousness because the weight of stress experiences during these years is intense, and made more so because this particular age group has few to no skills to deal with it. In fact, the PFC is still not fully mature, leaving the child and adolescent in a limbic world. For many children, the school experience is not always benign. Residual memories of particularly negative school experiences may still color the way some of you live your life today. For this reason it is imperative that all adults—teachers, parents, relatives, and friends—try to understand that much of this stress can be intercepted before it leads to trouble. The time to teach the stress-management skills that they can carry through life are during these formative years.

As someone who specializes in treating adolescents and teens, I see the emotional cost when our youth are not given help to understand and cope with their stress reactions in their daily lives. Too often, stress triggers in the form of family strife, academic expectations, and unrelenting peer pressure, lead kids down various roads of escape. Unfortunately, the routes that many teens choose are unhealthy, such as eating disorders and substance abuse. Mental health issues can arise, and in extreme cases, teen suicide. Approximately 4,500 youths between the ages of ten to twenty-four commit suicide each year, while about 150,000 show up in emergency rooms around the country because of the self-inflicted injuries of failed attempts according to CDC statistics.

The good news, however, is there are many ways to help kids feel less stressed out. One way, believe it or not, is via cell phone. While much controversy rages on the value of young people carrying cell phones, this device can serve as a direct avenue to kids' psyches, and parents can learn to take advantage of them with specific types of communication. Recent research at California State University on cell phone use between adolescents and parents suggests that cell phones could actually enhance relationships. Their research showed greater communication and closeness when it was the kids who made the call to parents, generally seeking support. However, when most of the calls were made by the parent to the child with the intent of monitoring activity or when upset, lower rates of self-esteem were reported among the adolescents. These results make sense. From the perspective of stress reduction, per-ceiving the phone as a support line would be much more effective in empowering the students than perceiving it as mainly a tool for supervision.

Teens and adolescents may view their phone as a support line on those occasions when they want to avoid an uncomfortable social situation without draw-ing the attention of peers. They can quietly text parents to be picked up someplace or give them an excuse to leave. Peer pressure in this age group can be intimidating and knowing there is a discreet lifeline of sorts can alleviate stress. The lifeline of course is not the phone, but the supportive voice of a parent who understands the sources of their adolescent's and teen's stress and who are willing to help them.

One of the biggest sources of school-age distress is fear of ostracism and of being bullied. For many young people, it is agonizing. But research shows that kids with strong family ties can better weather these challenges. Also, the belief that there will be change and/or justice gives youngsters strength to withstand ill treatment by peers. Researchers call this the Belief in a Just World (BJW) perspective, and international data shows kids who have faith in a just system had less distress. Parents, teachers, and other authority figures can reinforce this belief in youngsters. Instead of looking the other way and letting kids fend for themselves, they can send a clear message that bullying behavior will not be tolerated. In my own practice I see what can happen to adolescents who do not have anybody sending this message to them, and in the absence of belief in a possible good outcome, there lies only despair. A world of injustice is a world of every person for themselves. This is a recipe driven by cortisol.

Relationships and Respect

In all of our relationships we can help others stress less whether they're part of our inner circle or not. In turn we are reducing our own stress. The story at the beginning of this chapter is a good example of how we can be sensitive to another person's fears and anxieties— even if they are strangers. In doing so, we help them, and ourselves, succeed. Respect between human beings is an inclusive rather than exclusive concept. When we practice respect we are not only including and valuing others: we are giving them the benefit of believing that they are doing the best they can in that moment. This very act decreases their stress. Think about it. How many of us feel stress simply because we don't feel successful in the eyes of other people?

We all know people who go to great lengths to make a good impression. They do this so that they will be perceived as someone who fits in, or at the very least deserves respect. In some way, shape, or form, we all do this when we take a shower, shave, iron our clothes, and present ourselves as handsomely to the world as we can. So when we don't feel respected and instead feel alienated, the first thing we feel is stress.

But this is not just a phenomenon in modern, Western cultures. Recent studies among Amazon farmers revealed the very same reactions. Now, these are not people who generally use aftershave or wear Prada accessories to gain social acceptance. Each culture has its norms. Nevertheless, Spanish researchers found that the farmers who felt they were accepted were less stressed, less sad, less angry, less fearful, and happier and more successful than those people who felt like they were not living up to expected social behaviors. In addition, individuals who did not observe cultural norms were at a higher risk for both mental and physical illness.

Each of us at some time in our lives has felt awkward, uncomfortable, and that we didn't fit in. It is not a feeling any of us relish. But how often have we empathized with someone who seems to be feeling that they don't belong? We can help that person who may not quite fit in with the crowd by recognizing that they are still deserving of respect, still doing their personal best in that moment. This could be someone of a different social class, ethnic background, and educational level. Perhaps even someone with a mental illness. By showing respect we are telling them that they belong.

Respecting people is accepting people. When you do this, you are helping reduce your stress and theirs. Today, at home, what small thing can you do to make someone feel more successful, and more valuable? What about at work, or at school, or at the local store? We have in each of us the ability to decrease the stress in someone else, simply by seeing him or her as valuable, connected, accepted, and not alone.

chapter 11

The Future of Stress
and Epigenetics

We know from personal experience that the stress of someone else can cause stress in ourselves. A partner comes home from a tough day at work: stress. A kid comes home from a tough day at school: stress. Your boss takes it out on the employees, and sometimes they then take it out on others: stress. Stress can be thrown back and forth like a bad game of dodgeball. But did you know that stress can be passed down to the next generation? The stress you experience in your lifetime can be passed down through your genes to your kids. We call this new science and awareness, *epigenetics.*

All the techniques you have learned in this book to recognize and relieve your stress really can work. And as they do, you will be having an impact on some of the smallest parts of your body: Your DNA. Stress not only has a cultural component that can be passed on to children in the way they learn to handle stress. Stress also appears to actually change your biology, by changing your genes.

Most people have heard about genetics, and how the genes you inherit influence your eye color, height, the shape of your nose, and all sorts of things. Genes, as many people have learned, are discrete strings of DNA that have been linked together in unique sequences, and are wound securely around barrel-like structures called *histones*. These sequences of DNA, the genes, are wrapped and coiled tightly together in the famous double helix structure first described by James Watson and Francis Crick in arguably one of the most influential papers ever. The 1953 article published in the journal *Nature,* called "Molecular structure of nucleic acids; a structure for deoxyribose nucleic acid," was only 952 words, but changed forever our understanding of who we are and where we come from.

Since the discovery of DNA, scientists have been delving ever deeper into the mysteries of genetics. What they're learning is that certain of the genes we carry can be switched on or switched off. Sometimes these changes make us more susceptible to certain types of illness and disease. Sometimes they make us less susceptible. Quite recently, scientists have also identified potential DNA markers for the stress response and increased cortisol, making it another genetic trait lying in wait to be switched on—or not.

The news has become flooded with feature stories about the discoveries of various genetic markers for conditions like diabetes, breast cancer, and addiction. Yet, at the same time, we know that not everyone who carries the gene for allergies or obesity will actually become an allergy sufferer or grow dangerously overweight. Why not? After all, aren't the genes in charge?

In their quest to understand this mystery, scientists stumbled upon a most interesting and vitally important discovery: Sometimes the on/off signals are not inborn or inherited, but the result of influences from the world that we live in. Genetics is just part of the show, not the entire reason why we are who we are. This new knowledge has exciting, terrifying, profound, and promising implications. This is the power and promise of epigenetics.

Our environment can impact not just our own life experiences, but also influence the genetic legacy we pass on. The good news embedded in epigenetics is that we may be able to influence at least some of the traits we pass on to our children. Maybe not eye color, but perhaps a susceptibility to heart disease. Maybe not skin tone, but perhaps a resitance to obesity. Maybe not hair color, but perhaps the way we respond to stress. Epigenetics suggests that when we decrease stress in our lives, not only will it enhance our own health, but may in fact have a positive impact on the future health of our children.

Stress and Our Genes

For much of the past fifty years, it was thought that our genes were immutable entities. Nothing could change them except when new genetic combinations were made in reproduction, or the occasional mutation in copying that occurs by chance throughout life. Starting in the 1970s, scientists like Richard Dawkins, author of *The Selfish Gene,* suggested that it was the gene itself that dictated evolution, and that our bodies were merely vehicles to get those genes from generation to generation.

We know today that the story of our genes is much more intriguing, complicated, and adaptable than we ever imagined. In fact, our genes appear to be much more sensitive to the environment around us, and that environment may influence whether our genes will or will not activate. The combination of our surroundings and our genetic predisposition impacts us from the very moments we enter the world, and even in the womb itself.

From an evolutionary survival standpoint, it would

make sense for a child to be as genetically prepared as possible for the world into which they are being born. For instance, if you were living in a world where food was scarce, it would pay to have offspring that are able to efficiently use and store nutrients. Their chances for survival would be enhanced. But what if the environment they enter as infants is quite different from their ancestors'?

Such a scenario can be found among members of the Pima Indian tribe of Southern Arizona who suffer a higher-than-average rate of obesity and diabetes. Scientists from the National Institutes of Health have been studying the Pima DNA for more than thirty years, and have identified a gene, commonly found among Pima families, that causes the body to absorb more fatty acids from the fat in foods. Over centuries of surviving in sparse, desert conditions, this was an important trait.

Yet, over the last century this trait has not served the Pima, or many other groups, so well. Today, with plenty of fat-laden foods readily available and affordable, this particular gene has helped lead to insulin resistance and the development of diabetes. The good news, thanks to the Pima research, is that we now better understand this relationship between genes and the environment. For those who carry the family trait of diabetes, this increased awareness gives them the chance to control what they eat and how much they exercise.

Even if they are unable to prevent or delay that gene from switching on, a change in lifestyle can reduce the risk of those genetic influences having a deleterious effect.

In the case of stress, researchers are finding what they believe to be similar genetic patterns. Take for instance a mother who grew up in an environment where there was a lot of danger; a war zone perhaps. It would indeed pay genetically for her to have vigilant offspring with quick reflexes. But what if, instead of a world of fear and war, her child grows up in a world of relative safety and peace? That child may instead appear hypervigilant and see danger where none may be, simply because they have a gene switched on.

This applies to stress. Scientists have found that parents exposed to highly stressful and traumatic life experience have children who are at higher risk for developing PTSD. In compelling new research led by Dr. Rachel Yehuda from Mount Sinai Hospital in New York, studies are showing that adult children of Holocaust survivors were found to have greater levels of PTSD, even though they themselves had not been exposed to trauma. In numerous studies, these adults were found to have cortisol responses that were not in synch with the world around them. These children seem to have a heightened response to their own experience of stress. But why would these individuals experience symptoms of PTSD like anxiety, angry outbursts, and depression?

Indeed, one might think stories of war and violence could affect a growing child's psychology. But the degree of PTSD could not be explained by just hearing war stories. Some vulnerability appears to have been transmitted from one generation to the next, and the mechanism for this transmission is suspected to be epigenetics.

How Genes Get Switched On

The process of genes getting switched on and off is called *gene regulation*, and it is a critical part of normal development. Starting in the womb and throughout our lifespan, genes are turned on and off at specific times, to make sure that our eye cells look and behave differently than our knee cells. Not only do genes distinguish the type of cell, but genes also are regulated to be sure the cell is running as efficiently as it can and is working at the appropriate time. This cell regulation and activity is crucial to our well-being, and when it goes wrong it can result in potentially lethal consequences.

While bacteria or viruses that attack the body may cause disease, other diseases such as breast cancer or diabetes happen because a gene's code is switched on or off causing cells to function abnormally. These switches are regulated by information from the genes' environment, which activates proteins called *transcription factors*. When scientists test someone's blood and see an increase in transcription factors, it indicates genetic activity—even if a specific gene has yet to be identified.

In essence, these transcription factors are chemical machines that pull apart the DNA, and sit like a machine on the DNA strand. As this machine moves along the DNA it creates a mirror copy, called RNA. This RNA then has another protein machine sit on it, and transcribes that RNA into a sequence of amino acids. Amino acids form chains, connecting to each other like the beads of a necklace. These amino acid chains are the proteins, the enzymes, responsible for the actual activity of cells, carrying out tasks as diverse as getting sugar into cells (insulin), or taking out the cell garbage. Scientists used to think that these chains then folded onto themselves into firm and rigid structures. But exciting new research has shown that many proteins are actually floppy, pliable chains that can wrap themselves into different shapes, and thereby perform different functions. Mother Nature is frugal, and it would make sense that we have evolved an ability to conserve energy by making floppy protein chains that can do lots of different things: tools the cell will use to carry out the functions and needs of that cell.

While more and more has been discovered about

how DNA regulates cells, scientists have not yet been able to account for the precise controller of when a gene's code gets switched on or off, but they have been able to identify the traces of this action on the DNA. When a gene is in a *locked on* position, scientists have discovered that that gene has been *tagged* by a simple chemical structure called a *methyl group*. These tags are seen on the DNA of certain individuals who have inherited particular traits including disease risk.

For example, in certain types of breast cancer, scientists have identified a particular gene, the BRCA1, or breast cancer type 1 susceptibility gene, which is associated with a higher risk of developing this devastating illness. Research has shown that in women whose BRCA1 gene is methylated, the chance of having breast cancer was higher than in women who did not. These women are also believed to be more likely to pass on the methylated gene to their offspring—thus the epigenetic link.

In the case of intensely stressful life circumstances, many scientists believe that certain genes may be activated and in some individuals more likely to get tagged. Just as in breast cancer and many other diseases, the epigenetic journey of the stress response starts when that gene is first activated and marked for transcription.

Further Research

There's further evidence for the transmission of stress susceptibility coming from other research teams as well. Recently, researchers at Emory University may have encountered genetic activity of a family of genes involved in the stress response. In 2011, the researchers studied a group of women who had suffered extreme trauma, and also had a diagnosis of PTSD. They discovered that these women had higher levels of a specific protein associated with fear responses in the body; an increase in this protein points to the likelihood of genetic transcription. When running blood tests, they found two things. First, part of a particular gene was methylated, and second, the gene itself had a slight difference in appearance compared to women who had not suffered trauma. This study underlined the interplay between who we are and the environment in which we live; women who had a difference in the gene that coded for this particular protein were more susceptible to developing PTSD. And once such a trauma occurred, it appeared that the gene then methylated as a signal to enhance genetic transcription. Again, a potential epigenetic biomarker for PTSD.

It would make evolutionary sense that a stress gene might respond to environmental impacts even more quickly than other types of genes. This appears to be the case, as researchers at the University of Toronto have shown. Studying pregnant women exposed to high levels of stress, they've found repeated evidence that a mother's exposure to adversity during pregnancy can have lifelong effects on their children, and potentially multiple subsequent generations. While the Canadian's research focused on stress-response behaviors, and not on DNA, they also suspect these patterns indicate what they've described as *transgenerational epigenetic programming*.

Why is this important to know in a book about stress? Because the world we live in, and how we respond to it, can have an impact on the lives of our children. The more immediate implication of epigenetics is that the environment has an impact on us, right here and now. A gene is only as good as its environment, being transcribed or not depending on what the influences are on our brains and bodies. This means that in the course of a day we can have an almost inconceivable number of changes occurring at one of the smallest levels of our bodies, but with one of the largest impacts.

While we cannot always control stressful events going on in the larger environment, what goes on in our living rooms and kitchens is to a greater degree within our sphere of influence. The idea that we have enormous influence over each other is both common sense and startling. For with influence comes respon-sibility: What type of influence do you want to be?

Stress, Epigenetics, and Addiction

If you follow the epigenetic model, then the way you manage your stress is going to have an impact on your DNA. As you've been reading, there are both healthy and unhealthy ways to manage stress and each could potentially have an effect on your body, and the way your children handle stress. One unhealthy way many people deal with stress is through the use of drugs and alcohol. "Well, it's just one drink," or "Well, it's just weed," or "I'm only going to be on this Xanax or Va-lium for a short time." In this way we convince our-selves that using drugs and alcohol to deal with stress is a time-limited, and not a long-lasting problem.

This kind of thinking is not only self-defeating, but could not be further from the truth. More and more research is showing that the use of substances to allevi-ate stress may fundamentally be altering the brain, and not temporarily. One recent study from Mount Sinai School of Medicine suggests that drug addiction may stem from altering those parts of our brains involved in reward. The more the brain responds with pleasure to a substance, the higher the risk of addiction.

The irony is that while people use drugs to *feel* better, or *escape* from stress, epigenetics suggest we do not escape at all, but slowly build our own cages of dependence called addiction. And these cages are frequently passed on to the next generation. In my substance abuse program working with teenagers, many of the kids have parents who had their own challenges with drugs and alcohol. I do not think this is a coincidence, but know it is not a statement about morality: It could be the epigenetic consequence of an earlier generation's response to stress.

Think about this the next time you experience stress. That drink you have now to relax may have an effect on the actual DNA of your future kids. While guilt is hardly a stress reducer in and of itself, what you know about stress may be your key to reducing that stress and even heading off stress genes being switched on in your children.

Early Childhood Stress

Indeed, childhood may be the time when people are most susceptible to the environment and its impact on genes. Take the skin cancer melanoma, for example. One of the major risk factors for the development of this often deadly disease is three blistering sunburns before the age of eighteen. We don't need scientists to tell us that hard times in childhood can have an effect on kids, but we now know those stress-filled times actually have an impact on the *structure* of the brains of developing children. Of particular significance is the impact on the hippocampus, an area of the brain responsible for memories. We all have some childhood memories, hopefully mostly pleasant ones. But for children who were abused or under stress, those memories stored in the hippocampus can have an enormous influence on the choices that kid will make as a teenager and adult. Dangerous events lay down important memory tacks to enhance survival. Yet it is those memories that may drive behaviors, decades later. Early childhood stress is also associated with less activity of the PFC, suggesting that these kids are more emotional and reactive rather than thoughtful and able to use the skills inherent in the thinking part of our brain: certainly not a good thing for future stress control.

But it is not just these behavior challenges which concern scientists. It is when they occur, during periods of early development, which scientists believe is when genetic mechanisms may be most vulnerable to dysregulation and possible methylation of DNA. In recent studies, scientists in Zurich removed one-day-old mice from their mothers and observed that these baby mice had more behavioral difficulty compared to mice that had not been removed from their moms. These mice in turn had their own baby mice who displayed behavioral difficulty, despite their babies being raised normally. The scientists found that changes in DNA methylation were present in the brains of those second generation mice, showing that epigenetics has an influence from a single generation to the next.

While these studies often focus on the negative influence of the environment on our genetics, the flip side is quite encouraging. In the Swiss study, when the mice did not have stressful experiences, they had a reduced risk for gene methylation. In other words, we are not just slaves to the unrelenting, immutable destiny of our genes. A gene really is only as good as its environment. It will be turned on—or off—and regulated. This is where epigenetics can be such a cool thing to know about because in large part, how we create our environments is up to us.

Perhaps in the not too distant future we will find that all the things recommended to reduce stress actually have an epigenetic effect. It would make sense that meditation, mindfulness, psychotherapy, and other things we do in our daily lives to reduce our experience of stress probably have an epigenetic effect, reversing the first epigenetic effect or at least reducing it. It is in this elegant interplay of our human response to the world where we have a lot of power, control, and influence over the epigenetic experience of those in the world around us.

Conclusion

How can we apply this knowledge today, even in a small way? Use all the information in this book! Once we have identified the sources of our stress, and recognize that we all experience basically the same stress response, we can do something to relieve the stress in others. In giving back this way we not only help someone else, but we can see ourselves as more valuable and contributing to our home, community, and workplace. Even a simple "Thank you," to someone serving you a cup of coffee may reduce their stress, and potentially their entire day and epigenetic influence. Try it today. Say an extra "Thank you" as often as possible. The future of stress may be under your own control and your larger epigenetic influence.

Epigenetics may also pave the way for a deeper understanding of who we are, acknowledging the context of our experience and the knowledge that experience brings to bear on our lives. This powerful understanding gives us all a chance to see how much control we really have over our lives, and how very deeply we influence the lives of others. It is through our shared experiences that we can truly turn our stress into success, and use our entire evolutionary history to guide who we are and where we are headed. As I like to say: "The stress we share is more easy to bear." Working together we really can have the world in our hands, instead of carrying the burden of the planet on our shoulders. Working together we can turn our mutual stress into mutual success.

part VIII

References and Resources

chapter references

Chapter 1. A Response to Your World
Stress in America Findings, American Psychological Association, 2010.

Chapter 2. Biological Origins of Stress
Cannon WB. *Bodily Changes in Pain, Hunger, Fear, and Rage.* New York: Appleton-Century-Crofts; 1929.

Stawski RS, Almeida DM, Lachman ME, Tun PA, Rosnick CB. Fluid cognitive ability is associated with greater exposure and smaller reactions to daily stressors. *Psychology and Aging.* June 2010;25(2):330–42.

Stress Control: Techniques for Preventing and Easing Stress. *Harvard Medical School Report.* 2002. Dadoly AM (editor).

Yerkes RM, Dodson JD. The relation of strength of stimulus to rapidity of habit-formation. *Journal of Comparative Neurology and Psychology,* 1908; 18:459–82.

Chapter 3. Key Sources of Stress
Aman-Back S, Björkqvist K. Relationship between home and school adjustment: children's experiences at ages 10 and 14. *Perceptual and Motor Skills.* June 2007;104(3 Pt 1):965–74.

AP/mtvU Poll. Available at: http://hosted.ap.org/specials/inter actives/wdc/ap_mtvu_poll_0509/Content.swf. Accessed on 11.01.11.

Chandola T, Britton A, Brunner E, Hemingway H, Malik M, Kumari M, Badrick E, Kivimaki M, Marmot M. Work stress and coronary heart disease: what are the mechanisms? *European Heart Journal.* March 2008;29(5):640–8.

Cheng Y, Kawachi I, Coakley EH, Schartz J, Colditz G. Association between psychosocial work characteristics and health functioning in American women: prospective study. *British Medical Journal.* February 2000;3(20):1432–6.

Erath SA, El-Sheikh M, Hinnant JB, Cummings EM. Skin conductance level reactivity moderates the association between harsh parenting and growth in child externalizing behavior. *Developmental Psychology.* May 2011;47(3):693–706.

Essex MJ, Armstrong JM, Burk LR, Goldsmith HH, Boyce WT. Biological sensitivity to context moderates the effects of the early teacher-child relationship on the development of mental health by adolescence. *Development and Psychopathology.* February 2011;23(1):149–61.

Holt-Lunstad J, Uchino BN, Smith TW, Hicks A. On the importance of relationship quality: the impact of ambivalence in friendships on cardiovascular functioning. *Annals of Behavioral Medicine.* June 2007;33(3):278–90.

Ishak WW, Kahloon M, Fakhry H. Oxytocin role in enhancing well-being: a literature review. *Journal of Affective Disorders.* April 2011;130(1–2):1–9.

Kakihara F, Tilton-Weaver L, Kerr M, Stattin H. The relationship of parental control to youth adjustment: do youths' feelings about their parents play a role? *Journal of Youth and Adolescence.* December 2010;39(12):1442–56.

Saxbe D, Repetti RL. For better or worse? Coregulation of couples' cortisol levels and mood states. *Journal of Personality and Social Psychology.* January 2010;98(1):92–103.

Silver RB, Measelle JR, Armstrong JM, Essex MJ. The impact of parents, child care providers, teachers, and peers on early externalizing trajectories. *Journal of School Psychology.* December 2010;48(6):555–83. Epub September 17, 2010.

Chapter 4. Common and Mysterious Symptoms of Stress

Gonzalez O, Berry JT, McKnight-Eily LR, Strine T, Edwards VJ, Lu H, Croft JB. Current Depression Among Adults— United States, 2006 and 2008. *Morbidity and Mortality Weekly Report.* 2010;59(38):1229–35.

Porter C, Jones B, Evans C, Robinson C. A comparative study of arm-restraint methodology: differential effects of mother and stranger restrainers on infants' distress reactivity at 6 and 9 months of age. *Infancy.* May–June 2009;14(3):306–24.

Roth T. Prevalence, associated risks, and treatment patterns of insomnia. *Journal of Clinical Psychiatry.* 2005;66 (suppl 9): 10–3.

Schreck CB. Stress and fish reproduction: the roles of allostasis and hormesis. *General and Comparative Endocrinology.* February 1, 2010;165(3):549–56.

Chapter 5. How Chronic Stress Can Harm Your Health

Ader R, Felten DL, Cohen N, eds. *Psychoneuroimmunology.* 3rd ed. San Diego: Academic Press; 2001.

Broadbent D. *Decision and Stress.* London: Academic; 1971.

Carruth L, Jones R, Norris D. Cortisol and pacific salmon: a new look at the role of stress hormones in olfaction and home-stream migration. *Integrative and Comparative Biology.* 2002;42(3):574–81.

Choi J, Fauve SR, Effros RB. Reduced telomerase activity in human T lymphocytes exposed to cortisol. *Brain Behavior Immunology.* May 2008;22(4):600–5.

Cohen BE, Panguluri P, Na B, Whooley MA. Psychological risk factors and the metabolic syndrome in patients with coronary heart disease: findings from the heart and soul study. *Psychiatry Res.* January 30, 2010;175(1–2):133–7.

Holmes TH, Rahe RH. The social readjustment rating scale. *Journal of Psychosomatic Research.* 1967;11(2): 213–8.

Liston, C. Psychological stress reversibly disrupts prefrontal processing and attention control. *Proceedings of the National Academy of Sciences.* January 2009;106(3):912–7.

McEwen BS, Hatch H and Margaret M. Physiology and neurobiology of stress and adaptation: central role of the brain. *Physiological Reviews.* July 2007;87(3):873–904.

Masuda M, Holmes TH. The social readjustment rating scale: a cross-cultural study of Japanese and Americans. *Journal of Psychosomatic Research.* August 1967;11(2):227–37.

Ohira T. Psychological distress and cardiovascular disease: the circulatory risk in communities study (CIRCS). *Journal of Epidemiology.* 2010; 20(3):185–91.

Rahe RH, Mahan JL, Arthur RJ. Prediction of near-future health change from subjects' preceding life changes. *Journal of Psychosomatic Research.* December 1970;14(4):401–6.

Roemmich JN, Feda DM, Seelbinder AM, Lambiase MJ, Kala GK, Dorn J. Stress-induced cardiovascular reactivity and atherogenesis in adolescents. *Atherosclerosis.* April 2011; 215(2):465–70.

Spiegel B, Khanna D, Bolus R, Agarwal N, Khanna P, Chang L. Understanding gastrointestinal distress: a framework for clinical practice. *American Journal of Gastroenterology.* March 2011;1(106):380–5.

Suarez K, Mayer C, Ehlert U, Nater Urs. Psychological stress and self-reported functional gastrointestinal disorders. *Journal of Nervous & Mental Disease.* March 2010;198(3):226–9.

Woon TH, Masuda M, Wagner, Holmes NN. The social readjustment rating scale: a cross-cultural study of Malaysians and Americans. *Journal of Cross-Cultural Psychology.* December 1971;2(4):373.

Chapter 6. Healthy Responses to Stress

Lang EV, Large core breast biopsy: abnormal salivary cortisol profiles associated with uncertainty of diagnosis. *Radiology.* March 2009;250(3):631–7.

Chapter 7. Lifestyle Balance to Minimize Stress

Babyak M, Blumenthal JA. Exercise treatment for major depression: maintenance of therapeutic benefit at 10 months. *Psychosomatic Medicine.* September 2000;62(5):633–8.

Ditzen B, Schaer M, Gabriel B, Bodenmann G, Ehlert U, Heinrichs M. Intranasal oxytocin increases positive communication and reduces cortisol levels during couple conflict. *Biol Psychiatry.* May 2009;65(9):728–31.

Dusek JA, Stress management versus lifestyle modification on systolic hypertension and medication elimination: a randomized trial. *Journal of Alternative and Complementary Medicine.* March 2008;14(2):129–38.

Holt-Lunstad J, Social relationships and mortality risk: a meta-analytic review. *PLoS Medicine.* July 27, 2010;7(7): e10003162010.

Hölzel BK, Carmody J, Vangel M, Congleton C, Yerramsetti SM, Gard T, Lazar SW. Mindfulness practice leads to increases in regional brain gray matter density. *Psychiatry Research.* January 30, 2011;191(1):36–43. Epub November 10, 2010.

Light KC, Smith TE, Johns JM, Brownley KA, Hofheimer JA, Amico JA. Oxytocin responsivity in mothers of infants: A preliminary study of relationships with blood pressure during laboratory stress and normal ambulatory activity. *Health Psychology.* 2000;19:560–7.

Nakamura A, Fujiwara S, Matsumoto I, Abe, K. Stress repression in restrained rats by (R)-(–)-linalool inhalation and gene expression profiling of their whole blood cells. *Journal of Agriculture and Food Chemistry.* June 2009;57(12): 5480–5.

Seider BH, Hirschberger G, Nelson KL, Levenson RW. We can work it out: age differences in relational pronouns, physiology, and behavior in marital conflict. *Psychology and Aging.* September 2009;24(3):604–13.

Splevins K, Smith A. Do improvements in emotional distress correlate with becoming more mindful? A study of older adults. *Aging Mental Health.* May 2009;13(3):328–35.

Wallace RK, Benson H, Wilson AF. A wakeful hypometabolic physiologic state. *American Journal of Physiology.* September 1971;221(3):795–9.

Chapter 8. Creating a Stress-Reduction Plan

Kroll, C. Volunteering, Happiness and the "Motherhood Penalty." Paper presented at the "Volunteering Counts" conference. Manchester, UK. March 2010.

Powell ED, Albers J, Andry S, Greenlund E, Ojile JM. Does habitual stress cause sleep problems and daytime functioning impairments, or is stress the result of poor sleep? *SLEEP.* June, 2009; 8;32(suppl):1268.

Rose N, Koperski S, Golomb B. Chocolate and depressive symptoms in a cross-sectional analysis. *Archives of Internal Medicine.* 2010;170(8):699–703.

Chapter 9. Handling Severe Stress and Unexpected Stress Events

Brown CH, Bennett ME, Li L, Bellack AS. Predictors of initiation and engagement in substance abuse treatment among individuals with co-occurring serious mental illness and substance use disorders. *Addictive Behaviors.* May 2011;36(5):439–47.

Butler AC, Chapman JE, Forman EM, Beck AT. The empirical status of cognitive-behavioral therapy: a review of meta-analyses. *Clinical Psychology Review.* January 2006;26(1):17–31.

Crow SJ, Peterson CB, Swanson SA, Raymond NC, Specker S, Eckert ED, Mitchell JE. Increased mortality in bulimia nervosa and other eating disorders. *American Journal of Psychiatry.* December 2009;166(12):1342–6.

Dhalla S, Kopec JA, Ewing JA. The CAGE questionnaire for alcohol misuse: a review of reliability and validity studies. *Clinical and Investigative Medicine.* 2007;30(1):33–41.

Grant BF, Prevalence and co-occurrence of substance use disorders and independent mood and anxiety disorders: results from the National Epidemiologic Survey on Alcohol and Related Conditions. *Archives of General Psychiatry.* August 2004;61(8):807–16.

Hudson JI, Hiripi E, Pope HG, Kessler RC. The prevalence and correlates of eating disorders in the National Comorbidity Survey Replication. *Biological Psychiatry.* February 2007;61(3): 348–58.

Chapter 10: How to Become a Stress Expert

Correia I, Kamble SV, Dalbert C. Belief in a just world and well-being of bullies, victims and defenders: a study with Portuguese and Indian students. *Anxiety Stress Coping.* October 2009;22(5):497–508.

Ishak WW, Kahloon M, Fakhry H. Oxytocin role in enhancing well-being: a literature review. *Journal of Affective Disorders.* April 2011;130(1–2):1–9.

Lewis PS, Malecha A. The impact of workplace incivility on the work environment, manager skill, and productivity. *Journal of Nursing Administration.* January 2011;41(1):41–7.

Phillips T, Ferguson E, Rijsdijk F. A link between altruism and sexual selection: genetic influence on altruistic behaviour and mate preference towards it. *British Journal of Psychology.* November 2010;101(Pt 4):809–19.

Reyes-García V, Gravlee CC, McDade TW, Huanca T, Leonard WR, Tanner S. Cultural consonance and psychological well-being. Estimates using longitudinal data from an Amazonian society. *Culture, Medicine, and Psychiatry.* March 2010; 34(1):186–203.

Saxbe DE, Repetti R. No place like home: home tours correlate with daily patterns of mood and cortisol. *Personality and Social Psychology Bulletin.* January 2010;36(1):71–81.

Weisskirch RS. No crossed wires: cell phone communication in parent-adolescent relationships. *Cyberpsychology Behavior Social Networking.* January 4, 2011. Epub ahead of print.

Chapter 11: The Future of Stress and Epigenetics

Dawkins R. *The Selfish Gene*. New York: Oxford University Press; 1976.

Franklin TB, Russig H, Epigenetic transmission of the impact of early stress across generations. *Biological Psychiatry*. September 1, 2010;68(5):408–15.

Matthews SG, Phillips DI. Transgenerational inheritance of stress pathology. *Experimental Neurology*. January 31, 2011.

Maze I, Nestler EJ. The epigenetic landscape of addiction. *Annual New York Academy of Science*. January 2011;1216:99–113.

Ressler KJ, Mercer KB. Post-traumatic stress disorder is associated with PACAP and the PAC1 receptor. *Nature*. February 24, 2011;470(7335):492–7.

Watson JD, Crick FH. Molecular structure of nucleic acids; a structure for deoxyribose nucleic acid. *Nature*. April 25, 1953;171(4356):737–8.

Yehuda R, Bierer LM. Transgenerational transmission of cortisol and PTSD risk. *Progress in Brain Research*. 2008;167:121–35.

information resources

Find a therapist (www.4therapy.com)

Academy of Cognitive Therapy (www.academyofct
.org)

American Academy of Child and Adolescent Psychiatry (www.aacap.org)

American Association of Geriatric Psychiatry (www
.aagponline.org)

American Institute for Cognitive Therapy (www
.cognitivetherapynyc.com)

The American Institute of Stress (www.stress.org)

The American Psychiatric Association (www.psych
.org)

American Psychological Association (www.apa
.org)

The American Psychological Society (www.psycho
logicalscience.org)

Anxiety Disorders Association of America (www
.adaa.org)

Benson-Henry Institute for Mind Body Medicine
(www.massgeneral.org/bhi/default.aspx)

Internet Mental Health (www.mentalhealth.com)

National Institute of Mental Health (www.nimh
.nih.gov)

National Mental Health Association (www.nmha
.org)

Psychologically Healthy Workplace Program (www
.phwa.org)

Transcendental Meditation (www.tm.org)

Harvard University links

www.harvardhealthbooks.org
www.health.harvard.edu
www.health.harvard.edu/blog
http://twitter.com/#!/harvardhlthbks
http://twitter.com/#!/harvardhealth
http://www.facebook.com/pages/Harvard-Health
-Books/114327901985190
http://www.facebook.com/HarvardHealthPublica
tions

index